Anonymous

James Stephens

Chief Organizer of the Irish Republic

Anonymous

James Stephens
Chief Organizer of the Irish Republic

ISBN/EAN: 9783744760621

Printed in Europe, USA, Canada, Australia, Japan

Cover: Foto ©ninafisch / pixelio.de

More available books at **www.hansebooks.com**

James Stephens,

CHIEF ORGANIZER OF THE IRISH REPUBLIC.

EMBRACING AN ACCOUNT OF THE ORIGIN AND
PROGRESS OF THE

FENIAN BROTHERHOOD.

BEING A

SEMI-BIOGRAPHICAL SKETCH OF JAMES STEPHENS, WITH THE
STORY OF HIS ARREST AND IMPRISONMENT; ALSO HIS
ESCAPE FROM THE BRITISH AUTHORITIES

NEW YORK:
CARLETON, PUBLISHER, 413 BROADWAY.
M DCCC LXVI.

PREFACE.

A "BIOGRAPHY of James Stephens" cannot yet be written, for his life has not yet terminated, and his work is not accomplished. Nor can the "History of Fenianism" be indited while the freedom of Ireland from British rule is an unaccomplished fact. He who shall write the one, must necessarily indite the other. At the present time, a brief sketch of the work performed by the one, and the progress made by the other, may serve to throw some light upon the condition of Ireland and assist in her redemption.

There will, doubtless, be found some inaccuracies in this little book, but the material points of which it treats are substantially correct. In the absence of any official records to which to refer, the author has been compelled to rely mainly upon oral statements, and the current newspaper reports of the day for his facts. By condensing, sifting, and collating these, he has striven to write as near the truth as possible.

There are some faults of omission as well as commission in this narrative. While there are yet a hundred thousand Irishmen in their native land, who have been identified with the recent revolutionary movement there, it would be manifestly improper to relate the facts which would compromise them and subject them to penalties provided by English law.

Conscientiously using the material within his reach, the author has endeavored to deal fairly with all parties interested. That his efforts may contribute towards developing among Irishmen in America a pure and holy sympathy for their unfortunate country, and serve to persuade them to more united efforts, is his most fervent wish.

NEW YORK, *May 28th*, 1866.

INTRODUCTION.

IRELAND—HER GRIEVANCES AND HER PROTESTS.

THE few pages which are to introduce a brief sketch of the life of the latest Irish conspirator, and the story of the organization of which he is the head and heart, are addressed less to Irishmen, than to those whose idea of Irish grievances is indefinite —to those who, with but a vague knowledge of either the country or her wrongs, and an imperfect one of her people, yet leap at the wish to set her free of English rule, more from an intuitive knowledge that freedom is her right, than from conclusions forced upon them by familiarity with her history. And to that other class, by individual members of which the question is often asked, "But what has Ireland to complain of now? is she not an integral portion of the British empire, duly represented in its government, and sharing in its influence and progress?" To these it ought to be enough to say, "read Irish history;" more than enough to say, "you cannot get these two nations to work smoothly together; fire and ice are scarcely less congenial; centuries of experimenting have failed to discover the affinities; centuries of subjection and efforts at amalgamation have failed to break down the barriers dividing them." The English and the Irish people remain this day as distinct in each characteristic feature as any two nationalities in existence. The Irish have within themselves all the elements of independence, all the elements of becoming a useful if not a powerful member of the family of nations. It can be no longer doubted that it is the wish of this people to be independent; they struggle for it, and are discontented failing to secure it. What American can withhold his respect for that discontent? Freedom is this people's right, and this alone ought to be argument enough for the wisdom of their discontent.

If a people through successive generations fail to appreciate the beneficence of a government which, in the first instance, was forced upon them, and ever since sustained by brute force only, opposed to their solemn and reiterated protest, and in defiance of repeated outbreak (whether all this be a result of their ingratitude, their obstinacy, or their want of appreciation of the blessings of such obtrusive friendship, it matters little); it must be accepted as evidence of the want of that integrity of parts so necessary to the peace and prosperity of a nation as a whole.

To all students of Irish history, it is known that there is no chapter there unmarked by protest in some shape or other against English rule; not a few of them written in the blood of the malcontents; in fact, the only history that Ireland has to show for centuries is the story of her successive protests against what she takes the liberty to call the usurpation of her government by English rulers. Let us sketch in a sentence or two the story of these protests.

With the presence of Strongbow on Irish soil began the struggle between the English and Irish people, lashed into fury at times, with periods of calm intervening, for over four hundred years. Then came the conquest of the gentle Mountjoy, who boasted that he gave to his no more tender-hearted mistress "a country of carcasses and ashes." A period of churchyard silence here succeeds, but a resurrection follows it, and the tongue which is spoken is still the language of the Celt. Elizabeth gave place to James, and James to Charles. Charles gave his head to Cromwell. The English people were under the iron heel of the Dictator, but the Irish, the resuscitated Irish, were in rebellion! Again the spoiler was upon them. This time the work of devastation was complete; fire and sword had sway unlimited; lands were laid waste; homesteads pillaged, and, in the name of God, the followers of Cromwell possessed themselves of Irish maids, and lands and gold, and made her rich soil richer still with the blood of her slaughtered sons. This time she is not only dead but buried. Before, like the son of the widow of Nain, she had arisen from the bed of death. This time she is entombed. But even from out the grave, dug by the swords of merciless soldiery, she once more emerges; the stone is rolled away for her resurrection, and she stands again to battle for her nationality. She protests once more against England's rule and England's king, and fights with a broken sword against William of Nassau and his hireling soldiery. This time she is not beaten, but she capitulates, and the treaty of Limerick is signed. For the right to worship God after the fashion of their fathers, the Irish laid down their arms. With or without arms they still protest. The father who succumbed begat sons to whom he left the legacy of his hate. The English, no more faithful then than they are now, and the record of their truthfulness is fresh upon our memories, taking advantage of the first symptoms of another protest, broke through the sworn-to treaty, and enacted through their tools in the so-called Irish Parliament the accursed penal laws, the prominent features of which may be written as follows:

Catholics were excluded from every profession except the medical, and from all official stations without exception.

Catholic children could only be educated by Protestant teachers at home, and it was highly penal to send them abroad for education.

Catholics were forbidden to exercise trade or commerce in any corporate town.

Catholics were legally disqualified to hold leases of land for a longer tenure than thirty-one years, and also disqualified to inherit the lands of Protestant relatives.

A Catholic could not legally possess a horse of greater value than five pounds, and any true Protestant meeting a Catholic with a horse worth fifty or sixty pounds, might lay down the legal price of five, unhorse the idolater, and ride away.

A Catholic child, turning Protestant, could sue its parents for maintenance, to be determined by a Protestant Court of Chancery.

A Catholic's eldest son turning Protestant reduced his father to a tenant-for-life, the reversion to the convert.

A Catholic priest could not celebrate mass under severe penalties; but he who recanted was secured a stipend by law.

That this code wrought long and well is a well-known story. This monster, begotten on Irish soil, a lineal descendant of the Reformation, a child of the "glorious revolution," did its work bravely. As Burke says of it: "It was a machine of wise and deliberate contrivance, as well fitted for the oppression, impoverishment, and degradation of a people, and the debasement in them of human nature itself, as ever proceeded from the perverted ingenuity of man."

It did its work bravely indeed. Hear how the seventeenth century ended:

"The manufacture of wool into cloth had been totally destroyed by law. Acts of the British and Irish Parliament (the latter being wholly subject to the former) prohibited the export of woollen cloth from Ireland to any country whatsoever except to England and Wales. The exception was delusive, because duties amounting to a prohibition prevented the Irish cloth from entering England or Wales. Before that time Ireland had a good trade in woollen drapery with foreign countries, and undersold the English Therefore the British Parliament addressed King William, urging him to suppress the traffic. The House of Lords used this language: 'Wherefore we most humbly beseech your most sacred Majesty that your Majesty would be pleased, in the most public and effectual way that may be, to declare to all your subjects in Ireland that the growth and increase of the woollen manufactures there hath long been and will be ever looked upon with great jealousy by all your subjects of this kingdom, and if not timely remedied may occasion very strict laws totally to prohibit it and suppress the same.' King William, the Deliverer, replied that he would do his utmost to ruin his Irish subjects. 'He would do all that in him lay to discourage the woollen manufactures of Ireland;' and he was as good as his word.

Now, for a hundred years, Catholic Ireland is gagged; but she still protests against British misrule with the Protestant tongues of Swift, and Lucas, and Molyneux. It was not necessary for the mother to be Catholic that hate for England might mingle with that mother's milk; it was only necessary for her to be Irish. English cupidity, and the monopolies born of it, did their work; the country was impoverished; the people were swept to their graves by the thousand. No coroner's jury tells the story of their dying, but it is written in a language as indelible as the stars—"starvation."

The century drew near its close; a generation had passed away without a sign. The Protestant element was a strong one now, but it was Irish Protestant. The thunders of Napoleon's cannon were echoed by the cliffs of Dover—England was in danger. Protestant Ireland was appealed to, and she answered with eighty thousand bayonets. The Frenchmen did not come, and the bayonets were no longer needed. But in the meantime, "England's difficulty was Ireland's opportunity." The star of the unhappy land rose above the horizon for an hour. Backed by these eighty thousand bayonets, an independent parliament made laws in College Green, and for a space she gloried in her ancient title of the "Sovereign Kingdom of Ireland." Then upon Irish cannon was the motto, "Free trade or else"—that free trade meaning the right of the Irish people to regulate their commerce as best suited Irish, not English, interests; the right to levy duties for the support of an Irish, not an English, government.

For eighteen years the Irish people rejoiced in

an independent government, obeyed the laws which emanated from the Parliament at Dublin, and prospered under the protection of its paternal care. Manufactories sprang up again. The proverbially discontented Irish gave respectable evidences of a love of industry and of the good things purchased by its exercise. The agricultural produce of the country found a home market in exchange for native manufactures. Fat cattle ceased to crowd the ships for English shores, and broadcloth ceased to be a heavy inward freight. The public revenues were expended at home. Dublin grew beautiful in public buildings, this day her pride and shame. Landlords began to stay at home and spend their rentals there. The beautiful city on the Liffey was sufficient attraction for the most fastidious, when she bore the prestige of independence.

But could this state of things last? Could England afford to lose so good a customer for her manufactures, so good a market wherein to buy her beloved beef? Could she afford to permit a rival shopkeeper at her very door, who, a short time before, had been her customer, but now threatened to share even her foreign trade, if not, from peculiar facilities of manufactures, drive her completely out of the markets where she had hitherto held monopoly? Of course not. The rival shopkeeper must be crushed, not by honest competition; no, that would be a tedious and uncertain process; but by any and every means her innate selfishness could devise by which to effect her object. With eighty thousand muskets to protect her neighbor's trade, she dare not attempt to drive her from the

market. No, but she would kill her with kindness.
Every concession was made; all that Ireland asked
was given; England was for the first time her true
and tender-hearted sister. Now the time was
come when the peaceful relations of the world,
and especially of these two loving sisters, asked
for the disbanding of this great army of Irish
volunteers. The English standing army was sufficient for protection of the "Sister Islands." The
confiding Irish believed the story, and the volunteers were disbanded. This was the initiatory step
to the "Act of Union." But the proposed union
was unpalatable to the people. Even a corrupt
Parliament, which might be cleansed some day, in
Dublin, was better than a sixth of the representation in the London one. The scheme, however,
which began with the disbanding of the volunteers
could not end there; the union must be accomplished. The premature rising of '98 was brought
about. By what villanies generated and how
fomented is but too well known, as is the story of
the sacrifice which left its blood-stain upon many a
threshold. England had conquered once again;
terrorism was rampant; public meetings were dispersed by the soldiery; the national press was
bribed; a muzzled and a hireling one lied its utmost;
the Irish Parliament was packed with English
instruments, and by corruption and intimidation
the Act of Union was carried.*

The twenty years which followed were twenty

* For the *modus operandi* by which this Act was brought to a
successful issue, read the black list appended to Sir Jonah Barrington's "Rise and Fall of the Irish Nation."

years of prostration of spirit, of lingering death to manufacture, of concentration of all power in England, and of an exodus from Ireland of that wealth which, expended at home, had given stimulus to trade and confidence to the people. Gloom and poverty settled down upon the land, till 1817 found the people again dying of starvation. Many of the inhabitants of the Western and North-western coasts dragged out a miserable existence on seaweed, and to thousands potatoes were a luxury; the people died by wholesale of famine-fever, not in the poorer districts only, but in the best counties in the country. During this famine and that of 1822, and the intervening years, most strange to stay, the English peasant throve and fattened; there was no fever cloud to fling its shadow over his happy fields; English looms were busy and her artisans were fed.

What! had Providence stricken Irish fields with barrenness in condemnation of her near-sightedness? Had it cursed her with famine for her folly? No; strange to say, there was neither murrain among the cattle nor a blight upon the wheat, but the poor of the towns were unemployed; there was food, but not the means to buy it. English looms were musical, Irish looms were rotten with disuse. The petty manufactures had followed the greater ones, and shops were closed, for the customers had gone, and the money with them, to the theatres of power and place in England. No, there was no dearth of food; a loaf might be had for sixpence, as in preceding years, but there was no sixpence to buy withal. In 1817 there were exported to England from Ireland over 700,000 quarters of grain alone, and vast herds of cattle; and in 1822, over one million quarters of grain. Did the money come back to Ireland for all this? Oh, no; it stayed in England to pay the rent, or followed to the Continent the landlords who had forsaken their homes, and entrusted the paternal cares of their estates to the management of their agents and their tenants to their mercy. On the debate in the House of Commons in 1822, William Cobbett, an honest Englishman, writes in this fashion:—

"Money, it seems, is wanted in Ireland. Now people do not eat money. No; but the money will buy them something to eat. What! the food is *there* then, pray observe this, reader, pray observe this, and let the parties get out of the concern if they can. *The food is there*, but those who have it in their possession will not give it without the money. And we know that the food is there; for since this famine has been declared in Parliament, thousands of quarters of corn have been imported every week from Ireland to England."

The records of this time alone are so accursed that could Irishmen forget the tyrannies of six hundred years preceding, their hopes of vengeance dare not perish whilst this one memory remains. Starvation in the midst of plenty. Persecuted thus in body, as they had been in spirit for centuries; famished in the midst of fruitful fields, and their souls restricted under penalty to orthodox devotion, did they drop upon their knees and cry peccavi? prostrate themselves and place their necks within the English halter? Oh no! they had not done *protesting* yet.

Then was the birth-time, among the moderate and the cowardly, of the Catholic Relief Agitation, and amongst the more earnest, because most suffering, of Ribbonism and the Society of the Whiteboys.

Catholic emancipation was conceded to the former in 1829; and this concession to the manes of their fathers, who tasted the first rigors of the penal laws, and of the hunted priests who died by them, satisfied for a time the sick at heart, but failed to bring a soothing balm to the bulk of the people, in whom the music of their church bells, heard for the first time in centuries, could not drown for ever the dying groans of the massacred and the famished that filled up the space between.

It is known the part which O'Connell took in the agitation which led to the emancipation of the Catholics, as it is known the hold which from that time he had upon the affections of the Irish people. A period of rest now follows, or, what was worse, of peaceful agitation. The Precursor Society was followed by that organization, having O'Connell for its leader, and for its object the repeal of the "Act of Union." How O'Connell manœuvred the passions of the Irish people, and how he in turn was manœuvred and bepraised by that people's enemies, whose game he played, is a painful story within the memories of most of us. But there came a time when the people's heart grew sick with the hope deferred, for the "Repeal" which had been promised them as the fruit of each incoming session of Parliament grew no more certain as the years went by, but the ruin of the country grew more certain daily. The monster meetings of 1843, in the might of their *moral* strength, had failed to intimidate the English Government, and O'Connell was afraid (whether for himself or for the people, God knows) to use the power he held to awake that physical force which he might have controlled at will, and, as his countrymen then and now believe, directed to success.

But the paternal government was in action during all this time, in its own way, for Irish amelioration. Laws had been enacted disfranchising the holders of petty freeholds; their votes no longer available to their landlords, they were swept from their miserable homesteads by the thousand. To make ejectment in every shape of easy execution, laws unknown to the English Common Law were made and put in force, resulting in the desired consolidation of farms, and in the pauperism of the ejected. In 1846 the famine came, and the country was ripe for it; ripe for the harvest of death, and the reaper, Heaven knows, had a busy time of it. The story of that horror, the Irish famine, is as well known in America as it is in Ireland. A famine which swept into untimely graves a million people. A famine in a land from which had been exported the year before over $80,000,000 worth of produce to England; and in one day of the self-same year, 1847, shipped for the London market over eleven thousand quarters of wheat. From Newry alone, within five days, in the end of September, there sailed eleven ships for England laden with grain, exclusive of two large steamers, which sailed four times a week, laden with cattle, eggs, and butter. From Drogheda, that same week, were shipped 1,200 cows, 3,500 sheep and swine, 2,000 quarters of grain, 211 tons of flour and meal, butter, eggs, and lard. From Waterford, in the same week, 250 tons of flour, 1,100 sheep and pigs, 308 head of cattle, 5,400 barrels of wheat and oats, 7,700 firkins of butter, and 2,000 flitches of bacon;

and all the while the cry for bread arose on every acre. Parents, mad with hunger, struggled with their famished children for the morsel of food which charity or chance had brought them. Hundreds died upon their hearthstones without a cry. In many places, including entire villages, the living were too weak to bury their brethren who had died from hunger. On the island of Innisbofin, off the coast of Galway, may be seen this day, among the ruins of an old chapel there, and lying in a corner, a pile of human bones, the skeletons of those who were carried to that consecrated spot by the poor old priest of the island. There were not men enough on the island who were able to give burial to the dead. Along the coast of Conemara, the people lived for many months exclusively on seaweed and such fish as they were able to obtain. And so it was on the coasts of Donegal and Antrim. Even in prosperous Belfast, men and women quarrelled along the quays for the particles of grain—drippings from the bags of the cargoes of corn being delivered. In one authenticated instance, an infant was found seeking sustenance from the breast of its mother, who had died of hunger, and alone.

Starvation was checked by the munificent charity of America, and by the generous contributions of other nations. Still the people were swept off by tens of thousands by starvation in the midst of plenty, whilst those who were able, fled to America, aided in that effort by the instrumentality of their relatives here, or by the sale of the few acres which they owned, or of their lease, if they were fortunate enough to have one.

Those who remained, starving or approaching beggary or starvation, still solemnly protested. The cry for independence, as a cure for all their ills, rose loud and long above the shrieks of famine. The bubble of peaceful agitation burst about O'Connell's ears, and out of the ashes of the party agitating for Repeal sprang the "Irish Confederation." O'Connell died. The French Revolution burst upon startled Europe. The down-trodden nations of the world dreamed that the star of their redemption had arisen. The people of Ireland looked for a new Redeemer from the east! Revolutionary clubs were formed in every town and hamlet. The young men of Ireland, irrespective of creed, or the difference of opinion as to the means to accomplish their country's freedom, which they had hitherto indulged in, shook hands as brothers and prepared themselves for the coming conflict. Arms were purchased in considerable numbers, and smithies were busy night and day in the manufacture of pike-heads. Treason was taught openly in the speeches of Meagher, O'Brien, Martin, Traitor McGee, Mitchel and a host of others, and in the pages of *The United Irishmen* and *The Nation*. The peaceful Protestant north was armed to the teeth, guns and pikes were hidden among the brick-fields near the manufacturing towns and in hay-ricks throughout the country. The people were ripe and ready once again. Then came the counteraction of the government—the arming of the Orange lodges; the industrious spread of the story, through a paid press, that the purpose of the confederates was that of the communists of France—subversion of all order and religion. Regiments poured in from

England; artillery was paraded through the streets of Dublin. An act was passed by a large majority providing "that any one who should levy war against the Queen, or endeavor to deprive her of her title, or by open or advised speaking, printing, or publishing, incite others to the same, should be deemed guilty of felony and transported."

Then followed the arrest of O'Brien, Meagher, and Mitchel, on a charge of sedition. Unable to find a jury sufficiently venal for their purpose, the prisoners were discharged. Mitchel was again arrested, prosecuted under the new act, and, with a new packed jury, was convicted and sentenced to transportation. The day on which Mitchel was to be taken from his prison, in Dublin, to undergo his sentence of transportation, was to have been that for a general outbreak. But this was in May; the crops were in the fields, not in the haggards; and a rising, it was deemed by many, ought only to be made in the harvest-time, when the people could find sustenance on the field; in the food within their reach. The leaders of the party, therefore, advised the waiting to the harvest-time. They waited; but the delay was fatal. Taken at that hour when the true pulse of Ireland beat steadily; when the police were rebellious to the heart's core, and not an Irish soldier in the country who was not ready to turn his bayonet towards an English breast, the country would have burst into a flame, and Ireland would have profited by the best chance she had had for freedom in centuries. Whatever the result, that was her one great chance—she allowed it to pass her by.

Troops were poured in in additional numbers;

newspapers were suppressed; martial law was proclaimed; diligent search was made for arms in every direction; weapons were placed in the hands of northern loyalists. Conservative flax-spinners and manufacturers pledged their workmen against secret societies. The appliances to put out the fire were manifold and successful; for, when the harvest came, came with it the miserable failure at an outbreak, and, following it, the arrest and banishment of many of the leaders. So ended the *protest* of '48.

"Now, surely," said the critics, who had written up this drama and spoken in terms of praise or blame of the actors therein, as their pay or spirit moved them; "now, surely, these Irish will wind up their national performance with this last act, the last scene of which is sufficiently tragical for a respectable denouement." "Surely," cried the English taskmasters, "these whipped hounds will howl to kennel and obey the lash." "Surely," said the peaceful priests, "good people, you must see that God is not with you in all this thing; be peaceful, be contented. Have you not a college where your priests are taught some Latin, and learn to swear allegiance with the vow of celibacy? Have you not a National school system where, with a little fighting on our part, but a few of you are perverted, and the rest but gradually Anglicised? What, if you persist in being a virtuous and prolific race, have you not the privilege to take your surplus selves to America, and your blessed pastor with you? God bless us all! it might be worse. There was a time when it was worse. I tell you, there was a time when they would have shot me for saying mass, or for shriving the soul of a dying sinner; now I can say mass in the broad daylight, and you can kneel before me till my blessing, to reach you all, has to pass out through the open door, for you are too poor to build a house for God and yourselves and me, God help you. But this is a wonderful change, my children. Bless God, starve a little, and be contented."

For a time it looked as if the critics were in the right; the curtain seemed indeed to have fallen on the last act of the Irish revolutionary drama. Wily diplomatists in England and the representatives of English rule, and the recipients of English bribes in Ireland, the Castle Hacks in Dublin, and the city shopkeepers who scrambled for viceregal pence, and the Orangemen of the north, and the Irish gentlemen, with English names and English proclivities, who had invested capital in spinning-mills and looms and bleach-mills on the banks of the Lagan and the Bann, all these rubbed together their exultant palms and thanked Heaven (no they didn't, they never thought of Heaven), and congratulated each other at the death and burial of Old Ireland and of Young Ireland just consummated.

Now suppose we rested here, has not proof enough been given of incompatibility of temper as between this English and this Irish people to ask the world's verdict for divorce? Whom God hath *not* put together man may break asunder. What need to write grievances, which even the few Conservatives in Ireland complain of, to show the injustice of the one contracting party? But let us see if there remained not some cause of discontent for even those who loved not revolution, and ignored the proposition that their country was compelled to a relationship with another, which she hated, and who reciprocated the emotion. Yes, even these quarrelled at a state of things which had led to the loss by Ireland of her position as a manufacturing country, and to her absolute dependence on England for manufactures in exchange for her agricultural produce—and at the subjection of the people to a landlord class, of English descent and English affiliation whose first and last duty was the exercise of a perpetual drainage upon their tenantry, that they might spend the proceeds in that country of their affection (the rental estimated as paid to absentee landlords being about thirty millions of dollars annually), and that, as a matter of necessity, paid in the produce of the soil—and at the existence of a State Church, sustained by the presence of British bayonets (polished and kept in point by Irish taxes), only for the especial comfort of English clergymen, the younger sons of English aristocrats, or older ones, who, from deficiency in mental gifts, were supposed to be fitted for nothing better, and thrown into the well feathered bosom of the Church in Ireland—and at the collection and absorption of the revenues of Ireland by English officials, who, having amassed fortunes amidst Irish poverty, retired for their enjoyment to their native island, or their expedition to the Continent, giving place to others of their kindred to begin and end in doing likewise—and at the presence in the country of from twenty to fifty thousand British soldiers, a militia at the beck and call of the English Government, a police force of ten thousand men supposed to be loyal also, and supported by an over-burdened and impoverished people—and, to sum up, at the state of things to which all this gave rise, which, while they had no hand in it, in fact ignored it altogether, was a state of things these peace-preserving, patient, peaceful, conservative people did not like; we mean that state of feeling all around them which was fostered in secret societies, and which any day again might develop itself in outbreak and rebellion; in fact, a state of terrorism which they feared had assumed a chronic character, and which, alas! (said they) was ruinous to all projects for the development and industrial progress of the country. So those who were most content had, at least, all these things to complain of.

For a time it looked as if the priests were right, and that the people thought so. Submission to the powers that be, was a doctrine easy to preach and of easy practice, and the rendering unto Cæsar of the things that are Cæsar's was easy too, for there was but little to give him now, and he was kind enough to come and take it.

Well, it is now eighteen years since the protest of '48; what has been going on since then? Since then the happy Irish people have been flying from a country for which they have given some evidences of their affection, as if their God had left it; perhaps He has, and they have set out upon a pilgrimage to find Him.

The population of Ireland in 1846 numbered nine million souls; to-day it is estimated at four millions five hundred thousand. Of these, three millions have found a home in America; for the balance, and the natural increase unaccounted for, ask Ireland's guardians, and the Poor Law guardians, and the graveyards without walls (they are too wide for that), in Skull, and Skibbereen, and Connemara, and the ditches at whose side the starving wretches lay down and died in Donegal.

Whole villages have disappeared; homesteads which had stood for a hundred years or more have fallen in the south and west in every parish, and stone fences have been piled up from their ruins to keep in herds of sheep for the English market as of old, but tended this time by English or Scotch shepherds, and owned by English farmers. The whole agricultural portion of the country is becoming as rapidly Anglicised as the best diplomacy of England can effect for her this wished-for change.

America is now the hope of most of the peasantry; their only wish to rake out the dead ashes on their hearth-stones, leave the widow's and the orphan's and the exile's curse for the incoming tenant, and follow the star of their new destiny to the West.

And those behind, and who must remain behind, what of them? Those without the paltry means to pay their own and their wives' and children's passage, without friends on this side to give them help? What of those who take things as they come—good and bad—and make the best of them? What of those, and they are many, who would rather starve, or fight and die in Ireland, than live in Eden, if that Eden were unbounded by the Atlantic Ocean on the west, and on the east by the Irish Sea? What of those during these eighteen years, from '48 to '66? Are they beaten to the ground at last? Do they accept this state of things without a murmur? Did the last demonstration of discontent die a miserable death at Ballingarry? Did their last hope for Irish redemption pass away with the exiled confederates? Not so, by the immortal and rebellious memories of Fitzgerald, of Emmet, and of Tone! Not so, by the memories of the men of Forty-eight! As faithful as the shamrock to the soil is the seed of revolution!

There is still another protest; and its history is found in the following pages, linked with the name of Stephens. Whatever may be the immediate fortunes of the organization in which this protest has taken shape, whatever its trials and its sacrifices, and however long delayed the consummation of its purpose, let us hope that this indeed will be the last protest of the Irish people against English rule. Let us hope that out of the misunderstandings and divisions which have unfortunately arisen among Irishmen in America, a perfect union may be born, no less strong on account of their brief estrangement; and that plans of concerted action with their fellow-countrymen at home may be matured and brought to issue. The presence among Irishmen in America, who, however differing in opinion, have a common object in view, of the man whose whole life is one of sacrifice to his love of country, ought to smooth away all difficulties, and reunite in one common brotherhood all patriotic Irishmen of whatever creed or complexion of opinion. It is as difficult to see how uniformity of action is to be arrived at except through the instrumentality of this man, as it is to entertain the shadow of a hope for the immediate delivery of Ireland without union.

Irishmen in Ireland—those in prison there (some of them doomed to a long life's exile), those who, although not yet within the greedy grasp of English law, are surrounded by the snares of the spoiler, and those who wait with patient, hopeful hearts and ready arms the signal for united action—all look forward for their own and their country's salvation to the coöperation of their countrymen in America, with their envoy and chief, JAMES STEPHENS.

JAMES STEPHENS—FROM A PHOTOGRAPH BY CARJAL, PARIS.

JAMES STEPHENS.

HIS BIRTH AND EARLY EDUCATION.

JAMES STEPHENS was born in the beautiful city of Kilkenny, Ireland, in the year 1824. His father was a man of considerable intelligence, who, in addition to his yearly income for services rendered as clerk, was possessed of some small property. At a very early age, James manifested an unusual thirst for knowledge, and notably a wonderful aptitude for mathematics. His father took delight in affording him every opportunity for study. He required but little assistance from teachers, his active and inquiring mind readily seizing upon and comprehending the ideas laid down in the works of his favorite authors. From the age of sixteen to twenty-two he was leading the life of a recluse, going into society scarcely at all, forming but few acquaintances, and living solely with his books. He became thoroughly familiar with English literature, and also acquired great proficiency in the liberal sciences. His early love for mathematics had been amply encouraged, and he finally resolved to study Civil Engineering, and adopt that as his profession. He readily obtained a position upon the Waterford and Limerick Railway, where his genius and skill soon won for him considerable distinction.

It was about this time that Smith O'Brien became prominent as a revolutionary agitator. The English Government had become more arrogant and oppressive than ever, and Irishmen believed that the proper time had arrived to strike for Ireland's freedom. The early education of Mr. Stephens, together with his extensive reading, had tended to make him a thorough Republican at heart. His sympathies were all enlisted in favor of his suffering country, but his extreme youth had hitherto prevented him from taking any active part in the agitation then progressing. The revolutionary spirit of his countrymen was catered to by factious leaders, and there were divisions and dissensions in the ranks of the patriots. Mr. Stephens watched all movements with anxiety and apprehension, holding as yet aloof from all parties, and sanctioning the policy of neither; yet resolved to act when the proper time should arrive.

MR. STEPHENS JOINS SMITH O'BRIEN.

In 1848, Smith O'Brien's policy led to open hostilities, and Mr. Stephens hastened to join his gallant band. The means whereby he was introduced to that unfortunate patriot were peculiar.

Mr. Patrick Donohue, from Dublin, while visiting Kilkenny, conducted himself in such a manner as to induce certain club-men to believe that he was neither more nor less than a British spy. He was accordingly seized and subjected to a rigid examination. Being unable to give a satisfactory account of himself, it was resolved to send him direct to Smith O'Brien under guard. The person selected as custodian of the suspected individual was James Stephens. He accordingly started for Cashel with his prisoner, and after much difficulty and many adventures, delivered him to the Revolutionary Chief in person. O'Brien was pleased with this exhibition of vigilance and zeal, and became speedily interested in Mr. Stephens. Finding in him a zealous patriot, an intelligent counsellor, and a thorough gentleman, he immediately attached him to his person as an aide-de-camp. The more severely the young man was tested, and the greater the responsibility cast upon him, the brighter shone his ability and his genius.

At the Widow McCormick's house, where the most serious outbreak of the '48 rebellion occurred, Mr. Stephens played a most conspicuous part, and from that day became a recognised leader of the people. On one occasion, during those momentous days of '48, at Killenaule, he, at the head of a few brave men, successfully defended a barricade against a troop of English horse, repelling their charge most gallantly.

It has been often reported, and is generally believed, that Mr. Stephens was wounded at the engagement at the Widow McCormick's house. This is a mistake. The rebels being defeated at this point, and scattered to the four winds, their leaders sought safety in a retired spot a short distance from the scene of the day's action. It was at this latter place where, after the reverses which had overtaken them, Smith O'Brien and his chief advisers assembled. They were now surrounded completely by the British soldiers, and there seemed little doubt that they would all be taken prisoners at daylight next morning. Here were Smith O'Brien, Michael Doheny, John O'Mahony, Bellew McManus, James Stephens, and a few other brave patriots whose names are dear to all Irishmen. A council of war was held to decide what was next to be done. The cause of Ireland had met with a deadly blow—the premature rising of a small handful of half-starved, unarmed peasantry, had ended in their complete rout, and consequent discouragement. The leaders appreciated the situation, and this council was to determine what should be their future line of conduct. By remaining together they would be sure to fall into the hands of their enemies, while by separating there seemed a possibility of their escape.

After consultation, all but two of these brave men decided that it was useless to pursue the outbreak further at this time, but that a few weeks must be allowed to pass by for the harvesting of the crops before further demonstrations should be made. The two who dissented from this policy were Terence McManus and James Stephens. They believed in action then and there, and volunteered to remain to the last with their chief, Smith O'Brien. The others determined to return to their several homes, and there keep alive the revolutionary spirit.

The parting of these leaders, as each went his way endeavoring to escape the eye of the British police, was very affecting. None expected to survive the dangers by which they were surrounded, and the "farewell" stuck in the throats of most of them. Mr. Stephens found himself the object of the kindest solicitude on the part of all, on account of his youth and the prominent and somewhat reckless part he had played. O'Mahony, particularly, displayed great interest in him, and gave him directions where to meet him again, and what route to pursue.

THE FIGHT, AND WOUNDING OF MR. STEPHENS.

Thus they parted; Smith O'Brien, McManus, and Stephens remaining where they were, the others departing by different roads. Mr. Stephens shortly learned that a body of police were on the road approaching the house. He being provided with a horse, persuaded O'Brien to mount; then taking from his head the plain cap he wore, exchanged it for the gaudy green and gold one worn by his chief, and entreated him to make sure his safety by flight. O'Brien took the advice of his devoted Aide, and bidding him good-by, hastened off.

Mr. Stephens then turned his own steps towards the approaching police. Falling in with ten or twelve fugitive rebels who had been defeated in the previous skirmish, he prevailed upon them to make a stand against the coming posse. He felt assured that if, even at that late hour, a small victory could be obtained, thousands would flock to his standard, and the rising would become general throughout the land.

The "peelers" advanced upon the rebels and were received with a volley from the few old muskets which they possessed. The pursuing body returned the fire, killing and wounding several of the patriots. Those who remained uninjured immediately scattered. Mr. Stephens was among the wounded. He had received one bullet through the fleshy part of the right thigh, and another had inflicted a contusion upon the left hip, which caused him great pain. Seeing his comrades flying in every direction, he attempted to get over a ditch, when he was saluted with another volley from the police, several bullets passing through his clothes. He fell as if killed, and the police passed on thinking him dead, and so they reported to their officers and the populace. After having bandaged his wound and made sure that it was safe for him to venture forth once more, the wounded leader started across the fields for a neighboring town. On his way he encountered a peasant, with whom he exchanged clothes to prevent detection.

FLIGHT OF STEPHENS, AND HIS VISIT TO HIS LADY-LOVE.

A little touch of romance saved him from being captured and sharing the fate of O'Brien, McManus, and others of his comrades. While following his profession, he had encountered in Tipperary a young lady whose bright eyes had made sad havoc with the heart of the youthful patriot. Now, wounded, weary, disheartened, and an outlaw, he resolved once more to seek his lady-love, and receive from her one fond adieu before seeking O'Mahony and his fellow-conspirators in their retirement. He knew the dangers he would encounter by the way; for the British soldiers and police were searching every nook and corner, and dragging to prison the unfortunate participants in the events of the past few weeks. But bright eyes lured him on, and he knew a hearty welcome awaited him in that distant town. And did he not have a beautiful precedent in the course pursued by one whose sorrowful history had ever been full of interest to him—the noble Robert Emmet, who, refusing to go on board the ship which was waiting to take him to sea until he should say good-by to the girl of his heart, was captured while receiving her last embrace, and was led away to prison and the scaffold? Having this bright example before his eyes, young Stephens set out upon his journey to Tipperary, having hired a cart to transport him. At one little town through which he passed on the same day he found the streets full of excited citizens. They had heard of the fight at the Widow McCormick's, and rumor having given the victory to the rebels, the people were anxious to join their brothers in the field. At their head was the parish priest, urging them to return to their homes and remain quiet. Mr. Stephens listened to the reverend speaker a few moments, and then approaching him, demanded the privilege of speaking to the crowd. The priest refused to listen to him, but denounced him as a spy. Thereupon the excitement became intense, and the denounced individual was in danger of being torn to pieces. At this critical moment a young man in the crowd recognised Mr. Stephens, and throwing himself in front of him, compelled the mob to listen to what he had to say. A few words sufficed to inform them of all that had occurred at the Widow McCormick's, whereupon a revulsion of feeling came over the crowd, and he was as near being killed by their kindness as he had been before by their pikes and scythes. The young rebel was carried in triumph through the streets, and finally sent on his way to Tipperary rejoicing.

2*

After many adventures and several narrow escapes from falling into the clutches of the vigilant police, Mr. Stephens reached the house of his lady-love. Here he passed three delightful days, receiving that kind nursing and watchful care which his wounded condition rendered necessary. But few visitors were allowed to approach the house, and nearly all those who were accorded that privilege were young ladies, whose sympathy for the wounded rebel would doubtless have kept him confined for weeks longer, had not his place of concealment become suspected. An Irish magistrate, whose meddling curiosity was of the Paul Pry order, having ascertained that a fugitive rebel was in his vicinity, set inquiries on foot which rendered the place too hot for the young and romantic enthusiast. He accordingly bade an affectionate farewell to the pride of his heart, and started once more upon his wanderings. Departing from his comfortable quarters, where youth and beauty had ministered to his wants, he slept that night in the open air beside a hedge, with a stone for a pillow.

From this time he shaped his way according to the directions given him by John O'Mahony, and soon joined that gentleman and Michael Doheny in their retired retreat. The report that Stephens was killed at the fight at Widow McCormick's house was generally believed, his friends doing their utmost to gain credence for it. His father aided in circulating the report, and even went so far as to get up a mock funeral for the unfortunate lad, and buried an empty coffin with all the honors. A little later Mr. Stephens had the pleasure of reading in the *London*

Times, a full report of his own funeral, written on the spot, "by our own correspondent."

His rumored death contributed much towards his escape from Tipperary, and finally from his native land. He nevertheless was compelled to use extreme caution in all his movements, and on more than one occasion was all his ingenuity called into requisition to enable him to escape the clutches of government officials. Arriving at the home of O'Mahony, he found it surrounded by the police. In company with that gentleman, however, he succeeded in evading their vigilance, and the two outlaws made their way to a small cabin on the mountain side, near Carrick-on-Suir, where they found Michael Doheny quietly awaiting intelligence of his friends. This patriot had also encountered many wild adventures during the few weeks just gone by, which have been given to the world in a book written by himself.

THE THREE OUTLAWS—STEPHENS, O'MAHONY, AND DOHENY.

On the morning following the events detailed above, the three conspirators—James Stephens, O'Mahony, and Doheny—for the heads of two of whom the British Government had offered a large reward—crossed the Suir before daybreak, and made their way to the Comeragh Mountains.

Here they spent several days, not daring to venture forth, or attempt to hold communication with their friends. A few trusted peasants alone knew of their retreat, and from these they derived their subsistence and their knowledge of passing events. While here, and living thus, outlaws in their native land, their footsteps dogged by emissaries of a government they loathed, these men resolved to devote their lives to the liberation of Ireland and the overthrow of the power of England. The revolutionary spirit of their countrymen was crushed out for the present, and the poor enslaved people had returned to the old ways, discouraged and demoralized. British rulers and British landlords were becoming every day more exacting and overbearing, but mismanagement, defeat, imprisonment, and famine, had so disheartened the people that no hope could be entertained of another rising at that time. A few years more must elapse, and new leaders, with more practical and more advanced ideas, must arise to inspire confidence in the hearts of the people. They must be organized. In the last days they had shown the proper spirit, but there had been no organization, and the people, when called to action, came forth as a mob, which could neither be used nor controlled. This must be remedied; the entire nation must be united in one mass of thoroughly drilled soldiers, before there could be any hope of a successful revolution. This was the feeling of Mr. Stephens as he and his companion pursued their lonely wanderings on Comeragh Mountains, and he resolved to bide his time. - But that such organization should be made, and another blow for Irish freedom struck, he not only firmly resolved, but to the accomplishment of that purpose henceforth devoted his life and his fortunes.

Great difficulty was experienced by Doheny and Stephens in their attempts to leave Ireland. So determined was the British government to secure the arrest of all who had been engaged in the late revolt, that patrols of soldiery and police were scouring road and field in their efforts to capture fugitives. Not a house, barn, or hay-rick in that portion of the country escaped search from the officers of the law. It finally became necessary for their own safety, that Doheny and Stephens should separate, and each in his own way endeavor to escape from their native land. They accordingly did so, and taking different routes, each strove to reach some Irish seaport town. After having encountered many adventures and hairbreadth escapes, Mr. Stephens reached Cork, without having assumed any disguise. By a strange coincidence, which did not end here, Doheny arrived on the same day, disguised as a hog-drover. Each, unknown to the other, engaged passage for England; they sailed on different schooners; left the harbor on the same day; arrived in England on the same day, and finally entered France on the same day, at different ports; neither, during all the time occupied in performing this journey, knew aught of the whereabouts or fate of the other, and it was not until nearly a month had elapsed after their arrival in Paris that they came in contact. Here, the resolves made upon the mountain were renewed, and each, in his own way, devoted himself to the accomplishment of the great object they had in view.

In an account of their trials and tribulations, which was afterwards published by Doheny in a volume (The Felon's Track), that distinguished rebel thus speaks of Stephens and the way he bore himself under the trying circumstances to which both were so long exposed:

"My comrade, who had no life to lose but his own, and who of that was recklessly prodigal, provided he could dispose of it to good account, stepped blithely along and uttered no complaint, although he left behind him traces marked with blood. His terrible indifference soon restored my self-possession, and we found shelter for the night. * * * * His imperturbable equanimity and ever-daring hope had sustained me in moments of perplexity and alarm, when no other resource could have availed. During the whole time which we spent, as it were, in the shadow of the gibbet, his courage never faltered and his temper never once ruffled."—*Extracts from "Felon's Track."*

While Doheny amused himself in writing ballads on such scraps of paper as chanced in his way, Stephens enlivened the tedious hours of their involuntary wanderings with song and jest. His spirits were high, and his fund of humor never exhausted.

MR. STEPHENS IN PARIS.

Mr. Stephens' hunger for knowledge had never been satiated, and knowing full well that he had much to acquire to fit himself to be a successful leader of a popular revolution, he immediately on his arrival in Paris again returned to his books. Shutting himself up in his own quiet room, he pursued his studies unremittingly, ignoring society almost entirely, and forming only such acquaintances as would contribute to the fulfilment of his plans. He was often cramped for even the necessaries of life, but by means of occasional services rendered to literary and professional friends, he obtained sufficient for his actual needs. For more than seven weary years did he remain in Paris, and nearly the whole of that time was devoted to his studies and in attendance upon lectures on the natural sciences, philology, and literature. He became distinguished as a linguist, being able to read readily in sixteen different languages. During the latter portion of his residence in Paris, he had contributed to the daily and weekly journals, his articles exciting much comment and admiration in the literary world. He also translated Charles Dickens' "Martin Chuzzlewit" into French, and had it published in that language. This added much to his literary fame, and contributed not a little to his purse. It has often been stated that during these seven years in Paris, Mr. Stephens became identified with secret political societies, whose object was the overthrow of the French government. This assertion is not true. While he lost no opportunity of familiarizing himself with the revolutionary leaders, and the principles and ideas which they advanced, he never was initiated into any of the secret societies. He was too much occupied with thoughts of his own unhappy country and in schemes for her delivery from the British yoke to become involved in the affairs of his neighbors.

STEPHENS SAILS FOR ENGLAND.

Early in 1857 he, believing the hour propitious for the commencement of those plans which he had been so long maturing, set out for England. His ideas of organization at this time were more comprehensive than ever before or since, and contemplated not only the liberation of his own native land, but the complete overthrow of British rule wherever found. To this end he proposed beginning his labors in London by the establishment of a daily newspaper opposed to the government, and republican in its views. He also sought to establish secret societies among Englishmen and Irishmen in England, to imbue their minds with republican ideas, and finally, to so spread the societies and the ideas that they should result in the overthrow of the British government at home and in all her provinces, and in the establishment of republican forms of government. After a short stay in London, however, Mr. Stephens' health became so bad that he was obliged to return to his native land, and abandon his plans. His severe study in Paris had made sad inroads upon his constitution. His medical advisers informed him that nothing but a speedy return to Ireland would save his life. Reluctantly he abandoned the field which had promised so fair a harvest, and in a short time again pressed the sod of his beloved isle.

HE GOES ONCE MORE TO IRELAND.

He allowed himself but a short time for rest, however. His was not a spirit to remain in idleness. His countrymen were being oppressed, impoverished, and driven by thousands from the land of their birth to seek the protecting shelter and the homes and liberty afforded them upon the soil of America. Positions of trust and emolument were offered him by those who feared his genius and his revolutionary spirit. They thought by tempting offers of pecuniary assistance to win him from the purpose he had espoused under such trying circumstances. All these attempts were persistently set aside by him, and he resolved to ascertain for himself, by personal observation, the state of the country and the sentiments of the people. Provided simply with his knapsack and staff, he started out upon this tour, nor did he return again until every town and every hamlet in the whole of Ireland had been visited. Alone and on foot he travelled from one extreme of the Island to the other, talking with the farmer, the peasant, and the laborer—sleeping in their cabins, and partaking of their poor and scanty fare. Their grievances were related and sympathized with; the farmer told how the landlord oppressed him, and how he took from him the last cent he could earn to pay the rent of a bit of bog and a leaky cabin, and how he was sometimes turned out of even that wretched home because he couldn't make enough from the soil to pay that rent. The laborer told of hard work and scanty pay. All complained of the rise of rents and the exorbitant taxes they were forced to pay to support a church and clergy they did not believe in. He found the old spirit of revolution still alive in their breasts; it slumbered, but was not dead. They were ready to strike for their freedom if only the proper leaders could be found, and the proper organization effected.

HIS TRAVELS IN IRELAND.

Mr. Stephens' travels afoot occupied him one year, during which time he traversed three thousand five hundred miles, and conversed with thousands of people—the bone and sinew of the land—under their own roof-trees. This journey rendered him more familiar with the condition of Ireland and the true sentiments of his countrymen than was any other person in the land. He returned fully satisfied that the time was ripening for the blow for freedom to be struck, and he resolved to prepare for it.

It was after this tour through the country that he first laid the foundation for the society which is now known as the Fenian Brotherhood. At that time he gave it no name whatever, but strove to render the organization so secret that the Government should obtain no clue even to its existence. The days of '48 had taught him that no revolutionary movement in Ireland could be successful unless the people were thoroughly organized, and each man sworn, by a solemn oath, to obey the orders of his leaders. In the days of John Mitchel and Smith O'Brien there were political societies, but no oath bound the members together. The consequence was, that a single priest could scatter a crowd of thousands simply with his denunciations. The people had to be educated to make a distinction between the priest in his capacity of religious instructor and the same individual as a politician. This was one of the objects of the society established by Mr. Stephens. The people recognised that their clergy were opposed to any attempt by battle being made to secure the liberties of the people. They must be taught that all due respect would be paid to them as priests, but that when they lent the dignity of their office to serve political ends, they put off the sanctity of the robe, and became as other citizens, and were to be treated as such. This lesson has since been well learned by Irishmen at home and abroad; and to-day the Fenian Brotherhood, which has been denounced by the clergy far and wide, embraces within its ranks two-thirds of the Irishmen of the world. Mr. Stephens established several of these societies, the members being sworn not only to watch over-the interests of Ireland, but to take up arms for her whenever called upon so to do.

At Skibbereen there was a political and literary association known as the "Phœnix Society." Most of the members of this society were enrolled by Mr. Stephens, but retained their original organization, designation, and outward seeming as a club, for the purpose of misleading the government in case its suspicions were aroused. A British spy, however, joined their order, and having mastered some of theit secrets, informed upon them. Many were arrested, and one conviction followed. The trials attendant upon the arrest of the Phœnix men created great excitement in the land. These patriots were called "Phœnix men" at the time of the prosecution, and for a long time the name attached itself to Mr. Stephens' secret organization, and it even became familiar in America.

ORGANIZATION OF LIBERATIVE SOCIETIES IN AMERICA.

In December, 1858, letters were brought to Stephens from Michael Doheny and other friends then in America, stating that their efforts to establish secret societies had been successful, and that an order was in existence here with the object of eventually affording relief to Ireland. These gentlemen desired him to undertake a similar organization at home, promising him such assistance from this side the ocean as might be deemed necessary. The experience gained by him during his pedestrian tour, and the favor which his embryo societies had met with, convinced him that the plan was feasible, and he so informed his American friends. He undertook to organize and enroll ten thousand fighting men in the space of three months, on the condition that he should have the supreme control of the revolutionary movement, and that the American auxiliaries should furnish him funds with which to meet the necessary expenses of such an undertaking. The first of these conditions Mr. Stephens insisted upon most strenuously. He was on the field where the action was to take place; he was to assume the responsibility of the movement; he was the chief conspirator, whose life would surely be forfeited if he fell into the hands of the British government. Assuming thus the responsibility and the risk, he demanded that his action should not be hampered by the dictation of men whose absence from the scene placed them in a position where they were incapable of judging of the necessities of the hour. His connexion with the movement in '48, and his subsequent studies and experience, had taught him that any conspiracy in Ireland looking to the establishment of a republican form of government, must not only be as secret as it could be made, to evade the eye of British officials, but must be governed and directed by one controlling mind.

His friends in America conceded this point, and while recognising him as the head and front of the revolutionary movement, promised to use every exertion to secure the coöperation of their countrymen here. Under these circumstances Mr. Stephens commenced his labor of organization. The societies already formed were visited and induced to extend their fields of labor; new societies were formed where none had previously existed, and the souls of Irishmen were once more filled with hopes of freedom. They responded nobly to the call of their beloved chief, entering into the societies with the full determination to take up arms in defence of their rights whenever called upon so to do.

SUCCESS OF THE NEW SOCIETIES.

In seven months Mr. Stephens had organized an army of thirty thousand loyal souls, who were sworn soldiers of the Irish Republic. So quiet and systematic had been his labors, that notwithstanding the fact that British spies swarmed in every town, the Government could obtain but little information regarding the organization. That secret political societies were in existence, was now well known, but their extent could never be ascertained; and England knew comparatively nothing of the formidable conspiracy going on under her very eyes.

From St. Patrick's day, the 17th of March, 1858, till the end of September following, Mr. Stephens devoted every hour to the task of perfecting this organization, and giving to it a military character.

FAILURE OF AMERICAN SUPPLIES.

His friends had promised to furnish him from America from £80 to £100 per month to enable him to complete his work; but the spring months passed and July came without bringing with it the remittances from across the ocean. Less than £100 in all was received by Mr. Stephens from the time he commenced the work of organization to the 1st of July, 1858. Meantime he had used in the work all the funds he had received or could raise upon his personal credit, and he was forced to behold the work of his hands about to be destroyed for the lack of that support which had been so confidently promised him. In this emergency he sent a trusted friend to America to consult with O'Mahony and Doheny, who were the representatives of the Irish movement in that country. These gentlemen were surprised to learn the extent of Mr. Stephens' organization, but could show no corresponding labor performed here. They, however, renewed their assurances of coöperation, but finally sent the agent back nearly as empty-handed as he came.

The result of this mission was exceedingly disappointing to Mr. Stephens and his co-laborers at home, but they were in nowise disheartened. Another long term of anxious waiting for the fulfilment of their dream of liberty must elapse, the impetuous ardor of their followers must be controlled, and they be taught that lesson of patience which their leader had been conning for ten weary years.

STEPHENS GOES TO AMERICA.

It was at length determined that Mr. Stephens should visit America, and for a brief period employ upon that soil the talent for organizing which had made him so powerful at home. Accordingly, in September, 1858, he landed in New York, and for the first time set foot upon those shores, where so many of his countrymen had found homes and fortunes. He was met by O'Mahony and Doheny, who extended to their old comrade a welcome as hearty as it was sincere. The young patriot was disappointed at the little progress his friends had made in laying before his countrymen the true state of Ireland. These two men, so brave in action, so ready to lead their squadrons in the field, who never flinched when death stared them in the face, who laughed defiantly when the British government fixed a price upon their heads, were found unequal to the task of eliciting that sympathy for their enslaved countrymen which Irish hearts, wherever found, are so willing to pour out in substantial form, when properly approached.

Mr. Stephens met many warm and influential friends of the cause in New York, but these gave so gloomy an account of matters here as to almost deter him from further efforts. But he felt the responsibility which rested upon him, and knew that thousands of anxious hearts at home were beating in unison with his, and that thousands of good and true men looked to him as their leader, and were watching his every movement with anxious eyes. He resolved, in spite of all opposition which was in his way, to commence and carry to success an organization here similar to the one in Ireland. O'Mahony, Doheny, Michael Corcoran, and a few other prominent and patriotic individuals seconded his efforts, and the movement was commenced; the late Brig.-General Michael Corcoran being the first man sworn in on this side of the Atlantic. But already nearly four months of precious time had elapsed since his arrival in America—time consumed in vain efforts of others to do what he had contemplated—and his countrymen were clamorous for his return to Ireland. Having at length gained the consent of his friends here to proceed in his own way, he started upon a tour through the States, leaving the organization in New York in the hands of his friends. His efforts met with success everywhere. Being a plain-spoken, energetic, and convincing speaker, he was listened to attentively, and his counsels followed.

The societies which he established were secret in their nature, and while they contemplated the liberation of their native land from British tyranny, the means he proposed to accomplish that end were different from those contemplated by the home organizations. There, every member was a soldier; here, each member was a contributor to the support and equipment of those soldiers. Mr. Stephens devoted only one month to this effort, and at the end of that time had established societies in many of the principal towns in the United States. Having received their assurances of hearty coöperation, and having raised some means, he returned to New York, preparatory to embarking for his native land.

HE IS RECOGNISED AS THE REVOLUTIONARY CHIEF.

While waiting in New York, the delegates of the societies he had organized drew up a document conferring upon him the sole control of the Irish revolutionary movement, and recognising him as the head of all Irish organizations throughout the world. Not alone in Ireland and America had the spirit of revolution taken root, but the sons of Erin in England, Australia, South America, and, in short, all over the globe, had become alive to the necessities of the hour, and were prepared to play their allotted rôles in the coming hour of peril. All united in recognising Mr. Stephens as their leader, and to him intrusted the control of the cause so sacred to them. Knowing full well the responsibility thus put upon him, he boldly accepted the trust, confident of his ability to accomplish much, and to at least develop the power and strength of his people.

With this feeling, and under these circumstances, he returned to Europe, his arrival being the signal for renewed hope throughout the land.

STEPHENS AGAIN IN PARIS.

Not caring to return to his native land until he had the means of accomplishing his work ready to his hand, he again proceeded to Paris, where he spent two weary years waiting for that assistance which never came. Meantime, he was in constant communication with the Societies on both sides of the Atlantic, urging the one to renewed efforts in behalf of their oppressed country, and to the other holding out hopes of coming succor. But the directors of Fenian affairs in America did not make that exertion among their countrymen which the emergency required, and the organization which had promised so much became paralysed and dead to all intents and purposes. The cry went up, "Why do not the Irishmen at home do something for themselves?" from men who should have known that Irishmen at home were shackled hand and foot with British fetters, and could make no movement for their relief until their more fortunate brothers in foreign lands furnished them the means of breaking their bonds. For this they prayed, and this had been promised. Those men who asked why Ireland consented to remain in fetters, never asked themselves, "Where is the assistance we promised? Where the guns, the bayonets, and other munitions of war we were to furnish?" They preferred to quietly fold their hands and complain that others did not do that which they themselves had stipulated to accomplish.

The entire sum of money sent to Mr. Stephens from America during the first six years following his efforts in 1858 did not exceed £1,500. Had it not been that Irishmen at home, from their own pitiful savings, contributed ten times that amount, the revolutionary spirit could not have been kept alive one single year—it would have died a natural death from want of encouragement.

During all the years which have passed since Mr. Stephens devoted his life to the cause of Ireland, he has never, up to the present time, applied to his own use one dollar of the amount contributed to secure the freedom of his native land. Not only has he refused to defray his own expenses from the public funds, but he has contributed thereto from his own slender means until £8,000 have been swept away from his private purse, leaving him greatly in debt to a few kind personal friends, whose confidence in the individual could never be shaken, whatever they might think of the cause he had espoused.

The indifference of Irishmen in America having for the time destroyed all hope of securing Ireland's independence, Mr. Stephens returned to Dublin and quietly awaited the course of events. Never for one moment, since the days of O'Brien and Mitchel, has he doubted the practicability of the undertaking when the proper moment should arrive. He had seen one or two opportunities for a revolutionary movement in Ireland, when England was in trouble elsewhere, pass unimproved because the Irish people were not organized. He had determined that this should not occur again, and that when the occasion for another rising came, his countrymen should at least be prepared to avail themselves of it. He therefore worked night and day in perfecting what then had no name, but what is now known as the Fenian Brotherhood. He had at this time established societies all through the land, but they were not sufficiently advanced to suit him. He accordingly visited them all, worked with them, added to their numbers, and watched them drilling as soldiers.

PECULIARITIES OF THE FENIAN ORGANIZATION.

The organization was a military one, somewhat peculiar in its formation. First, in each district a good and trusty man was selected by Mr. Stephens to act as an organizer. This individual was called a "Centre," his military rank being similar in power and duties to our colonel. This Centre then organized "Circles," each Circle comprising from 50 to 150 good and reliable men, who were presided over by captains. These, however, instead of being recognised by their military titles, were designated "A's" and "B's", the captains having authority to appoint sergeants, corporals, etc. It was provided that if the Centre was captured, the senior captain should immediately take his place, his vacancy being filled by the one below him, and so on throughout the whole society. Whatever office became vacant, for any reason, the next officer in rank below immediately took the place. By this means the Circles were never without a Centre, and when arrests were made of the leading men, it was found that the machinery was in nowise clogged. The Circles had their regular meetings and their military drills at stated intervals. A large number of the Fenians belonged to the militia, and were only too eager to avail themselves of the opportunity to instruct their brothers in the manual of arms. Indeed, so completely Fenianized did the militia of Ireland become that the British Government at length prohibited their drilling at all, and would scarcely allow them to assemble on the usual holidays.

DEATH OF TERENCE BELLEW MCMANUS.

In 1862, an event occurred calculated to convince every one that the representations which Mr. Stephens had made regarding the strength of the Fenians in Ireland were in no way exaggerated. This event was the arrival at Cork of the remains of that noble patriot, Terence Bellew McManus. It will be remembered that McManus was one of those devoted men who remained stedfastly with Smith O'Brien in '48 to the very last. He was eventually captured, while attempting to leave the country, and after suffering a long and tedious imprisonment, was brought to trial. The evidence against him was conclusive, and he was sentenced to be "hanged, drawn, and quartered," in accordance with the humane provisions of English law. This sentence was commuted, however, and he was doomed to spend the remainder of his days in penal servitude. While undergoing this imprisonment in Australia, frequent attempts were made by friends at home to induce the British Government to pardon him and the other patriots who were then pining in the penal settlements. McManus, however, stedfastly refused to consent to his name being used for any such purpose; he intended, if he could escape, to repeat his attempts to overthrow the British Government, and he would not place himself under any obligations to a power he hated, by accepting from it a pardon. He eventually escaped, and made his way to San Francisco, where he engaged in business. His name was always revered by his countrymen, not only for his unflinching bravery in the hour of danger, but for his undying hatred of the oppressors of his race, and his stubborn rejection of all overtures for pardon. In 1862, he died in that city, and his many friends decided upon sending his remains for interment to that Green Isle for which he had suffered so much.

When the body reached New York, his countrymen flocked in thousands to pay to it their last tribute of respect; and notwithstanding the fact that Archbishop Hughes had forbidden the members of the Catholic Church to participate in any demonstration on the occasion, the funeral cortège was one of the largest ever seen in New York. Thence the body, accompanied by a suitable escort, was conveyed to Cork. Up to this time, there had been very little known about the Fenian Brotherhood; and as the friends of Ireland abroad doubted its strength, Mr. Stephens consented that its members should contribute their share in paying fitting tribute to the illustrious dead. On the day of the arrival of the body in Cork, that city was filled with Fenians, who had been called thither by their chief. When the funeral escort came on shore with their dead leader, the body was received by a committee of distinguished gentlemen, and conveyed to a suitable place, where it lay in state for eight days and was visited by thousands. At the end of that time, the remains were sent to Dublin, and eight thousand Fenians formed in procession and accompanied them to the depôt. Sixty thousand more lined the sidewalks, remaining reverently uncovered as the last earthly remains of him they loved so well were carried past.

There was a continuous grand ovation all along the line of road over which the remains of this revered patriot passed from Cork to Dublin. At every station Fenians had congregated, and the occasion was one of the deepest solemnity throughout the land. When the obsequies were celebrated in Dublin, one hundred and fifty thousand participated in the demonstration, thirty thousand of whom joined in the procession. From these demonstrations the fact became at once apparent to the English Government as well as to the friends of Ireland at home and abroad, that there existed in the Green Isle an organ-

FENIAN BROTHERHOOD. 55

ization of sufficient strength to shake the power of England, if so inclined.

It had been thought by some Irishmen in this country that the arrival of the remains of McManus in Ireland would be a favorable opportunity for another revolutionary attempt. They accordingly sailed for their native land at the same time, and immediately commenced agitating for a rising. In some localities they found many followers, and had hopes of being successful. Indeed, even Fenians who were bound to Mr. Stephens had become impatient of delay, and were willing to unite in any movement which promised even the shadow of success. But their chief knew that the hour had not arrived; the spirit of the people might be ripe for revolution, but they had neither arms nor means to prosecute it to a successful issue. He accordingly communicated to the Centres of his Circles that no outbreak would be allowed at that time, and the attempt of the American patriots was frustrated. At several places, however, Fenians had congregated in large numbers, ready and willing to do anything, expecting that the word for action to begin would be given. At one place upwards of a thousand stalwart Fenians had collected at the depôt, awaiting the arrival of the train which was bearing the remains of McManus. They had been informed that when the train arrived there would be work to do, and they were prepared to undertake anything. One of the foremost, acting as spokesman for the rest, sought out Mr. Stephens, and inquired what was to be done. He directed them to form in line quietly, and then having gained a position where he could be heard, and in a voice

which once heard is to be obeyed, shouted to them,
"To your knees, men! to your knees, every one!"
Instantly every knee was bent, and every head
reverently uncovered. In this attitude they remained, murmuring heartfelt prayers, until the train
bearing the corpse of their hero had passed. Quietly
then they dispersed to their several homes, content
to pay the tribute of a tear to the memory of the
dead patriot, and to obey the commands of their
living chief.

STRENGTH OF THE FENIANS IN IRELAND.

At this time, out of a population of 5,000,000
people, 50,000 could be relied on to shoulder their
muskets and take the field against British oppression.

The amount of labor required to perfect this organization can only be appreciated by those who
have had some experience in organizing revolutionary movements. But at the head stood Mr.
Stephens, steadily guiding the Brotherhood in all
its affairs, and so perfecting the organization that
when the moment arrived for them to strike for
freedom, the British government should find, instead
of the undisciplined mob which had before been so
easily put down, an army of veterans, capable of
establishing their rights at the point of the bayonet.
He was personally known to but a few of the more
prominent Centres, yet his name was held in such
reverence by the masses that it was never allowed
to pass their lips for fear they might betray him.
He was spoken of as "the captain," and to say to
them that "the captain" wanted this or that done

was to secure its prompt performance. Even the Centres themselves whispered his name only when barred doors shut out all possibility of its being heard by watchful spies. Notwithstanding Mr. Stephens was known to so few of the members of the Brotherhood he was familiar with them all. Under different names and disguises, he visited every Circle frequently, often addressing them with encouraging words from "the captain" or superintending their drills.

THE ADVISORY COMMITTEE—FATE OF THE MEMBERS.

Several of the best and most intelligent men were selected by him as a Council of Advisors, to whom were submitted all questions of importance and whose opinions guided the actions of their Chief. The subsequent fate of three of the members of this council is well known. John O'Leary, Charles Kickham, and Thomas Clark Luby, gentlemen connected with *The Irish People* newspaper, were arrested on suspicion of being connected with a revolutionary conspiracy. An agent of John O'Mahony's having been sent to Ireland with despatches, was unfortunate enough to lose them. The documents fell into the hands of the British Government, and the arrest of hundreds of patriots followed. The investigations resulting from this unfortunate affair showed O'Leary, Kickham, and Clark to be identified with the conspirators, and their conviction followed without delay. They are now (June, 1866) serving out a sentence of twenty years' confinement at Pentonville prison, near London.

ANOTHER AGENT SENT TO AMERICA.

The vigilance of the police now rendered necessary an increased expenditure of funds in behalf of the Brotherhood. The treasury was exhausted, and the few moneyed friends of the cause had already been taxed to their last dollar. He had to assume the entire responsibility of weathering the storm which hung over the organization, acting at once as its financier and chief director.

In this emergency, he again sent to America a true friend of the cause to ask once more for that assistance which had been so often promised. This agent soon reached New York city, where he was met with glowing accounts of the progress of the Brotherhood all over the country. He, however, made a tour through the States, visiting many of the large cities, and addressing large assemblies of his countrymen. He thought everything looked favorable, more favorable than had been represented; but he was deceived. Machinations were immediately set on foot to counterbalance the favorable impressions he had made in the country by those who were loath to see any Fenian contributions leave the country. The mission of this agent was a failure.

Again was Mr. Stephens disappointed, but not disheartened. Difficulties beset his path on all sides, but his undaunted spirit never for a moment quailed before them. Fertile in resources, his mind no sooner realized the failure of one project, than another was suggested. Means to carry on his revolutionary enterprise must be obtained. Could he at this time, or at any subsequent period, have obtained the privilege of appealing directly to the masses at home with that freedom which is allowed in this country, he could easily have derived from his poverty-stricken countrymen the sums required to prosecute his plans for their liberation. But mass-meetings, which in this country are the means of direct personal appeal, were denied to him; and that mighty engine of Republicanism—the Press—was closed against him. He resolved, therefore, upon attempting the establishment of a newspaper in the interests of the Brotherhood, which should not only be instrumental in enlightening his people upon the subject so dear to their hearts, but should at the same time be made a source of revenue to their depleted Treasury.

ESTABLISHMENT OF THE "IRISH PEOPLE."

Accordingly, in 1863, he, by appeals made to the various circles in Ireland, succeeded in raising a sufficient sum to commence the publication of *The Irish People*. It freely discussed all matters touching the welfare of Ireland, and was devoted to the dissemination of Republican ideas. The paper was well edited, there being engaged upon its editorial staff several able and accomplished journalists; while its corps of contributors numbered in its ranks some of the most brilliant writers of the Irish race. Ten thousand copies of the first number were printed, and so great was the demand for it that the edition was speedily exhausted. The second and third numbers met with similar success, and it bade fair to meet all the expectations of its founder. But with the third number came trouble. Its tone was offensive to British tastes, and the government objected to its progressive views. It was denounced as seditious in its tendency and revolutionary in its teachings. Its circulation was opposed by the government and the clergy; and the opposition to it was sufficient to prevent its yielding that pecuniary profit which had been anticipated. On the contrary, for a portion of its existence, it was an expense to its founder, and he was called upon to contribute largely to its support from his private means. It survived, however, until 1865, when the finding of the documents lost by O'Mahony's agent showed it to be identified with the revolutionary party, whereupon the government seized upon and confiscated its presses and material.

THE CHICAGO CONVENTION AND FAIR.

In the winter of 1863 and 1864, the American Fenians began to take some very decided steps; and a Convention was held at Chicago, Illinois, for the purpose of consulting in regard to the prospects of Ireland, and attempting to hit upon some plan of action which should lead to a more extended and practical form of sympathy being adopted by the Brotherhood throughout the United States. This Convention was attended by delegates from all parts of the country, but more particularly from the Western States. It was in those States that the greatest strength of the Brotherhood was manifested at that time. Many schemes were proposed, some of which were destined to exercise a very strong influence over the future action of the American Brotherhood. Personal ambition on the part of several of the leaders had already manifested itself, and the struggle for power was here commenced. It was at this Convention that the idea of rendering the American Brotherhood independent of the organization in Ireland was first publicly broached. This Brotherhood had heretofore been considered auxiliary to the home society, and had recognised James Stephens as the head of the widespread movements for the liberation of Ireland. At the Chicago Convention it was contemplated to reverse the order of things, giving the American Brotherhood the supremacy, with power to dictate what should be the policy pursued by the people at home. In accordance with this idea, John O'Mahony was chosen President of the Brotherhood, and a Central Council chosen, which was to advise with the President on all affairs of importance. This was a direct blow aimed at Mr. Stephens and his Irish organization, the result of which was to give birth to all the unfortunate if not fatal dissensions which followed.

It had been determined to hold a grand Fair at Chicago, Illinois, for the benefit of the Brotherhood. Previous to the opening of the Fair, Mr. Henry Clarence McCarty was sent to Ireland, ostensibly for the purpose of procuring articles for exhibition and sale at the Fair. He was cordially received by Mr. Stephens and his friends, who seconded his efforts in every possible way. The office of *The Irish People* was made a depository for articles intended for this purpose, and the columns of the paper devoted to the advocacy of the scheme.

STEPHENS' SECOND VISIT TO AMERICA.

The great object of McCarty's trip was, however, to induce Stephens to visit America for the good of the cause, and especially that he might save the organization from threatened dissolution. He yielded to the representations made, and, as before stated, arrived in New York in the latter part of March, 1864.

After a few days spent with his friends, Mr. Stephens proceeded to Chicago, where he arrived the second day of the Fair. He was greeted with the greatest enthusiasm by the masses, but beneath the apparent cordiality of the more prominent Fenians there lurked a feeling of chagrin at his presence. It is not our purpose to go into all the petty intrigues which were here developed; we will pass them by with the simple statement, that they were numerous, some of them dangerous, and that they bore the most bitter fruits at a subsequent period. The Fair was a great success in spite of (or rather because of) the opposition to it, offered by the clergy of this country. The priests had objected to it from the first, and entreated their congregations to discountenance it entirely, threatening them in the most serious manner for any participation in it. The people, however, refused to be dictated to in this manner, and nearly 50,000 persons were present. It was here that Mr. Stephens learned, with feelings of regret and astonishment, that the American Brotherhood numbered only about 10,000 members, when he had been led to believe their numbers exceeded 50,000. He had in Ireland, where to be a Fenian was to be a conspirator, 60,000 active members of the organization, and he had hoped America would furnish at least an equal number. This statement was exceedingly discouraging to him, yet, upon certain assurances being made he promised that if England went to war that year on the Danish question, as was anticipated, the blow for Irish freedom should be struck on Irish soil before another year began. But if England should not go to war that year, he promised that the fight in Ireland should commence in 1865 at the farthest. This promise was a conditional one, dependent for its fulfilment upon assurances made him that the help required should be promptly furnished.

After the Fair was concluded, Mr. Stephens, saddened and somewhat discouraged at the prospect presented to him there, started upon an organizing tour through the West. He met with good success, and the encouragement given him in various cities served to remove from his mind the doubts engendered at Chicago.

STEPHENS ONCE MORE IN IRELAND.

He returned to Ireland in August, 1864, having realized £3,000 by his American trip; three times this amount had been assured him as an inducement to get him to come.

On arriving in Cork harbor, he found the country in a fearful state of excitement in consequence of the difficulties which were then in existence between the Orangemen and the Catholics. Several outbreaks of a serious nature had occurred, men had been killed on both sides, and it was feared that these demonstrations were but the forerunners of an open revolt. Mr. Stephens hastened to Dublin, to the great relief of his friends, and at once resuming the leadership of the organization, prevented the Fenians taking any part in the troubles. He found the organization deeply in debt, and was compelled to at once expend nearly every dollar he had brought back from America to liquidate claims which had accumulated during his absence.

PREPARATIONS FOR ACTION.

The Danish question was still a mooted one in Europe, and Mr. Stephens exerted all his energies in preparing Ireland for the commencement of hostilities in case England should be drawn into a war with any other power. Believing that "England's difficulty was Ireland's opportunity," he made every preparation calculated to secure the success of the contemplated revolution. But disappointment awaited him; no European war occurred, and, what was still worse, no help came from America. Instead of the money and munitions of war which had been so lavishly promised, all the assistance received from America by him to the end of January, 1864, was the paltry sum of £394.

In January, 1865, another Convention of the Brotherhood in America was held at Cincinnati, and to them Mr. Stephens appealed by letter for the fulfilment of the promises made to enable him to begin the fight in that year. He asked that for the first three months of that year he should

FENIAN BROTHERHOOD. 65

be furnished £1,000, the same amount for the month of April, and for May, June, July and August, £2,500 per month. He represented that this assistance would enable his countrymen at home to take the field before the winter months arrived. His arrangements at that time were such that with the sums mentioned he could have introduced into Ireland all the war material required. This was promised him, and the first instalments sent over; but subsequently the remittances became irregular, and soon ceased entirely, before one-quarter of the amount promised had been transmitted.

MORE DELEGATES SENT TO IRELAND.

In July of that year (1865), instead of sending the assistance promised, two delegates were sent to Ireland by the Brotherhood in America, for the purpose of inspecting the work of Mr. Stephens, and ascertaining whether a revolution was practicable. Mr. P. J. Meehan and P. W. Dunn were the gentlemen selected for this purpose, the former bearing the credentials of both from John O'Mahony. They sought out Mr. Stephens, made known the object of their visit, and were afforded every opportunity for fulfilling their mission. They soon expressed themselves entirely satisfied with the organization, and again assured Mr. Stephens that he should receive from America all the assistance that had been promised. It was at this time that it was agreed that the issue of Bonds of the Irish Republic should be entered upon immediately upon the return of Mr. Meehan to New York, and he promised to start in eight days.

These eight days were to be employed by Messrs. Meehan and Dunn in visiting some of their friends. At the expiration of fifteen days Mr. Stephens received letters from each of them, posted in different parts of Ireland, requesting him to send to them, *through the post-office*, the names of numerous Centres of Circles, expressing their desire to visit those organizations. Mr. Stephens, very indignant at such request, at once summoned them to Dublin, to confer about matters of vital importance. He received no answers to these summonses, and several days elapsed before Mr. Dunn returned. Mr. Meehan continued not only absent but silent.

SUSPICIONS OF TREACHERY.

The visit of Messrs. Meehan and Dunn to Ireland was the most unfortunate blow the revolutionary cause in Ireland had received in many a day. They had been provided with important documents—important only as they would, if captured, be found criminatory in their nature—and with funds for the use of the conspirators, which were in the custody of Mr. Meehan.

That gentleman, on the first day of his arrival, by some means lost everything in his possession belonging to, and giving information about the Brotherhood. The documents at once found their way into the hands of British police officials, and were the immediate cause of the wholesale arrests of Fenian leaders and sympathizers which have since been made.

For months previously British detectives, spies, informers, police, soldiery, and officials of every kind, had been endeavoring in vain to find out just what the documents lost by Mr. Meehan told them, viz. the prime movers of the Fenian organization.

These documents were simply the letter of John O'Mahony, endorsing Messrs. Meehan and Dunn, addressed to "James Stephens, Central Executive of the Irish Republic," and a draft for the sum of £500 drawn in favor of a respectable Irishman. This was the link, so long sought by the government, showing the direct connection between the revolutionary element in Ireland and the Fenian Brotherhood in America, and also giving endorsements to the sworn statements of Nagle, which statements otherwise, owing to the character of the man, would have been useless.

SEIZURE OF "THE IRISH PEOPLE" OFFICE.

Knowing James Stephens to be identified with *The Irish People* newspaper, on the night of the 15th of September the office of that paper was seized by the police, and its types and presses taken possession of by the government officials. At the same time a posse of police surrounded the house of one of its editors, Thomas Clark Luby, and patiently waited for the appearance of that gentleman. Two messengers, who were dispatched to him from *The Irish People* office during the night, were seized by the vigilant officers. Finally they entered Mr. Luby's house and seized that gentleman and a large lot of documents relating to the Brotherhood. These papers being calculated to implicate many people in the conspiracy, had been previously kept in a place of safety together with many private papers belonging to Mr. Luby. Anticipating just what had occurred, the seizure of *The Irish People* office, and the search of his own residence, Mr. Luby had brought the papers to his home for the purpose of destroying such as could be spared, selecting out his private documents and concealing the remainder where they could not possibly be found. It was while thus engaged that he was arrested. The papers thus found, placed in the hands of the police the names of many brave men who were connected with the Fenian organization, and led to their immediate arrest. But the first positive clue which the government obtained upon which to base an arrest was that furnished by the documents lost by Mr. Meehan. Without that the fatal discovery of the papers at Mr. Luby's could never have been made. It was freely admitted by British officials that all the information previously received by them had not been of a criminating nature, and the Attorney-General stated officially that without the Meehan documents no arrests could have been made.

The events immediately following the seizure of *The Irish People* office are of such recent date as not to require repetition here. How hundreds of brave and loyal Irishmen were seized and thrown into prison on suspicion of being Fenians; how Americans in Ireland were also suspected, arrested, and ordered to leave the country; how some of these patriotic men were brought to trial, and how nobly and defiantly they bore themselves; and how they were sentenced to years of penal servitude, are matters well known to the public.

REWARD OF £2,300 OFFERED FOR STEPHENS.

On the day following the seizure of *The Irish People* office—the 16th of September—a reward of £200 was offered for the arrest of Mr. Stephens. As days and weeks rolled on, and he still remained at large, this reward was increased publicly to £2,300; while privately it was known that whoever should produce in court the arch-conspirator, would receive from the Government and individuals an incredible amount. Yet while the ingenuity of the British Government was taxed to the uttermost to secure his arrest; while detectives were following every trail, and spies lurking in every corner—that gentleman remained quietly at his own residence in the suburbs of Dublin, pursuing his usual avocations.

HIS HIDING-PLACE.

In the preceding month of July he had rented for £60 a year (this is the *mansion* he is said to have occupied at Fenian cost!) a small house known as Fairfield, in the south-eastern portion of the city, near Sandy Mount, on the river Doder, and here he remained from that time until he was arrested. He was known there as Mr. Herbert, and was to be seen at all hours of the day, quietly digging in his little garden, indulging his refined taste in the cultivation of flowers, or bestowing a gardener's care upon the substantial vegetables which were destined to appear upon his dinner-table. The other occupants of this cottage were his wife, his sister-in-law, Charles Kickham, one of the editors of *The Irish People*, Edward Duffy, and Hugh Brophy. These gentlemen were all subsequently arrested.

It was believed that the excitement throughout the land, in consequence of the arrests, would lead to an outbreak on the part of the revolutionists. Indeed the hour was a propitious one; but that quiet country gentleman, in his suburban cottage, knew that, however ripe the times and the people might be for a rising against their self-delegated masters, the warlike preparations were not sufficient to ensure a success. An outbreak might be made in certain localities, and a temporary victory gained, but there was neither a sufficiency of arms nor ammunition in the land to warrant the slightest hope of success. Mr. Stephens knew this only too well, and bitterly did he regret that the promised aid from America had not reached him in time to enable him to take advantage of this popular excitement which seized upon every Irishman in the land, and aroused in him such deep indignation as to render him ripe for any deed that should promise to free his native land from the rule of the hated Saxon. The desire for the work to begin was so great in the ranks of the Brotherhood, that nothing short of the powerful influence which Mr. Stephens wielded over his countrymen and their devotion to him could have prevented an outbreak. That such was prevented when popular indignation was wrought up to its highest pitch, is an evidence of the high state of discipline to which the organization had been brought. The imperative order that no revolutionary movement should be made at that time went out from that controlling spirit, and was obeyed.

ARREST OF STEPHENS.

For over two months following the issuance of the proclamation setting a price upon his head, Mr. Stephens remained at Fairfield. A full description of his person had been published, and the police were in full cry after him. But few persons connected with the Fenian movement knew of his retreat, and the number who were familiar with his person was comparatively small. For seven years he had been a conspirator in Ireland, most of the time living in Dublin, yet his person was unknown to any policeman. His retreat was finally discovered, through the treachery of one who was familiar with the fact that James Stephens and Mr. Herbert were one and the same person. On the night of the 12th of November, Colonel Lake and Inspector Ryan, of "G" Division of the Metropolitan Police, with a large posse of policemen, surrounded the house at Fairfield, bent upon the capture of the great conspirator. Having placed his men so as to prevent any escape from the house, he at length entered the cottage and instituted a search for Mr. Stephens. Entering the sleeping apartment of that individual, the police found him quietly awaiting their approach, while his wife was still in bed. There he stood before them, yet none dared to arrest him. There is a provision of English law which prohibits an arrest being made unless the person arresting is sure of the identity of the person he desires to capture. Not a man of them was familiar with the personal appearance of him for whose arrest there was so much money to be gained.

This emergency had been provided for, and so complete were his precautions and foresight, that naught but the basest treachery could have given the authorities a clue to his retreat. At last some one cried out, " Where's Dawson ?" and that individual, a detective, having been summoned, proclaimed the identity of Mr. Herbert with that of James Stephens. He was at once taken into custody in the name of the Queen. Fifteen minutes elapsed from the time the police entered his bedchamber before the arrest was made. Mrs. Stephens bore the arrest of her husband bravely, and when they parted, asked his permission to visit him in prison. He replied: " You cannot visit me in prison without asking permission of British officials, and I do not think it becoming in one so near to me as you are to ask favors of British dogs. You must not do it—I forbid it."

The police, fully armed, soon started on their road to Dublin, having in charge Mr. Stephens and Messrs. Kickham, Duffy, and Brophy, the other occupants of the cottage who had also been made prisoners.

THE EXAMINATION.

By the time of their arrival in the city the police courts were open, and Mr. Stephens was immediately conveyed before Mr. Stronge to undergo a preliminary examination. The news of his arrest had spread throughout the city, and the excitement was intense. It was feared that an attempt would be made by his devoted admirers to rescue him from the hands of the police. The Prosecuting Attorney, Charles Barry, was present, and a distinguished lawyer volunteered his services in behalf of Mr. Stephens. This was most emphatically refused by him in that bold and defiant language which no person ever dared to breathe before in public in Ireland, and which caused the most profound sensation when heard. He said, addressing Mr. Stronge, "I have employed no lawyer, nor have I put in any plea in this case, neither do I intend to do so. By so doing, I should be recognising British law in Ireland. Now, I conscientiously and deliberately repudiate the rightful existence of British law in Ireland, and I scorn and defy any punishment it can inflict on me." The greatest excitement prevailed in the court-room in consequence of this defiant speech, and every man present felt that, in consequence, Mr. Stephens' doom was surely sealed. A few moments sufficed to conclude the examination, and the accused was remanded to prison for a further hearing. This occurred on Saturday; on the following Tuesday he was again arraigned, and then formally committed to Richmond Prison to await his trial before a Special Commission which had already been ordered to convene. The other prisoners who were arrested at his house were also committed for trial.

STEPHENS IN PRISON.

Mr. Stephens having been fully committed to await his trial upon a charge of high treason, found himself speedily locked within the walls of Richmond Prison. This prison, built of solid stone and surrounded by high walls, is considered the strongest and most secure place of confinement in Ireland. The four prisoners, Mr. Stephens, Brophy, Kickham, and Duffy, were escorted to the cells allotted to them. These were located on the second floor of the prison, and were at some distance from each other. The cell to the right of Mr. Stephens was untenanted, while the one between him and Kickham on the left was occupied by a convicted thief. This convict was employed by the Superintendent of the prison to assist in watching Mr. Stephens. A cord was fastened in his cell communicating with a bell in the Superintendent's office, and the convict, on hearing any unusual noise in the cell of the conspirator, or any attempt at rescue, was to give the alarm immediately. This spy testified, subsequently, that when the escape was finally effected, although he heard the noise, he dared not ring the bell for fear of being killed. Notwithstanding the fancied security of the prison, the utmost vigilance was exercised by all the prison officials to prevent the possibility of the prisoners holding communication with their friends. None but those enjoying the entire confidence of the prison officials were allowed to converse with them, and, with the exception of two hours per day, which were allowed for solitary promenade in the court-yard, they were securely locked within their cells. Aside from being so closely confined and guarded, they were treated with tolerable courtesy and kindness. During the early part of his imprisonment, Mr. Stephens had no hope of effecting his escape before trial, although his friends knew full well that the sentence which might be passed upon him could never be carried into effect. He knew that thousands of devoted followers stood ready and eager to do anything, even to sacrificing their lives, if necessary, to secure his release ; but he would not add to the complications in which they were involved by permitting them to make any demonstration in his behalf.

The excitement in Fenian circles, in consequence of the arrest and imprisonment, was most intense, and schemes for his rescue, some of which contemplated the destruction of the prison, were discussed far and wide. These plans were all put aside by the bold and skilful man to whom Mr. Stephens had entrusted the direction of affairs during his incarceration. This man was Colonel Thomas J. Kelly, formerly a staff-officer in the army of the Cumberland, who won his laurels and his promotion upon the battle-fields of West Virginia, Kentucky, and Tennessee. In April, 1865, Colonel Kelly, who, while still in the American army, had tendered his services for active work in Ireland, and who was then a tried and trusted Fenian, joined Mr. Stephens in Dublin, and during the few months succeeding his arrival, had displayed so much skill and ability as to win not only the confidence of his beloved chief, but the respect and good opinion of all the leading revolutionary spirits of the time. Colonel Kelly had resolved, from the moment that Mr. Stephens was seized, that he should never be brought to trial, and he took measures to enforce that resolve, as will be seen.

THE ESCAPE FROM PRISON.

The arrrest, as we have stated, occurred on the morning of the 11th of November, and a Special Commission had been ordered to convene on the 28th of the same month, before which the chief conspirator was to be tried. The plans of Colonel Kelly, to be of service, must be speedily executed, and that they were complete in every detail and successful in their result is already known.

The details of the escape of Mr. Stephens from Richmond Prison, and the names of the persons who assisted therein, cannot be given to the public in full until the Irish Republic shall be recognised among the nations of the earth, and those prisons, which have proved the tombs of so many noble patriots, have become portions of its possessions. It is a fact, however, that those who assisted in the escape were so completely masters of the situation, that for days they laughed to scorn all idea of their beloved chief being brought to trial. Indeed, the fact that he was to escape, and that the well-laid plans to secure his release would be put into effect on a certain night, was well known to the organization throughout the whole of Ireland, and had even been communicated to Colonel O'Mahony, in America; yet so perfect was the organization, and so devoted its members, that not a whisper of such purpose ever reached the ears of British officials. Sufficient details of this escape, however, can be given here without criminating those who assisted therein, and who are yet residents of their native land, to clear up somewhat the mystery which has surrounded this transaction, and which will, at least, have the merit of being truthful.

There were in Dublin many men, some of whom had previously been employed within the prison, and others who had been confined there, who knew all its ins and outs, all its highways and byways. These men were now Soldiers of the Republic, devoted to their Chief, willing to lay down their lives in his behalf, and sworn to obey the orders of the officers appointed over them. There were employés still in the prison, also, who were members of the organization, who were ready to connive at the escape of the Central Organizer. But he who rendered the most important service was a British official, high in office, who, for a stipulated sum of money, furnished to Colonel Kelly wax impressions of the various locks of the prison. These impressions were taken to a skilful workman, still in Dublin, and from them he was enabled to construct skeleton keys, so deftly made that when the occasion came to use them it was found that the prison-bolts yielded as readily to them as they did to those in the hands of the officials.

All arrangements having been made to the satisfaction of the Colonel, he, on the morning of the 24th of November, together with a few other bold spirits, repaired to the prison. It was a cold night; the rain fell in torrents, and the wind howled dismally through the almost deserted streets, as these few men hastened from different directions to the appointed rendezvous. The first thing to be done was to post sentinels at some distance from the prison, to guard all the approaches, to give the alarm if the movement was discovered, and to bring reinforcements to the scene if necessary. Colonel Kelly, while making the rounds of these sentinels, encountered a policeman in the vicinity of Love Lane, and that individual owes his life at the present moment, to the fact that his curiosity did not lead him to follow the person who was so quietly promenading the streets at that early morning hour. While skeleton keys had been prepared to unlock the doors leading from the prisoner's cell to the prison yard, it was well known that the outside gates were too well guarded to permit of their entering that way. But these men were fertile in resources. A rope thrown over the outside wall sufficed to enable two of them to climb to the top and lower themselves to the inside.

One of those who thus entered the prison had formerly been employed there, and knew all that was necessary to know to effect their purpose. It appears that the Superintendent of the prison had, a short time before, become exceedingly economical in his views, and had consequently reduced the number of watchmen within the walls. Only one at a time was now required to be on duty, and lest he should prove negligent, a tell-tale clock was put up at regular intervals, by means of which the high dignitary who introduced the reform could tell whether or not the watchman had made his rounds at the proper time. The tour of duty was performed in this manner: the watchman, on starting upon his rounds, performed upon the first dial the operation known as "pegging the clock," which showed the time he entered upon his duty. Passing along the corridors, he was required to try every lock, examine every door, and satisfy himself that every cell was occupied by the person assigned to it. At another point of his rounds, he encountered another tell-tale clock, which he was required to "peg" as he had the first, and so on throughout the entire prison until six clocks had been thus manipulated. The time occupied in making the rounds was one hour and a half.

The old employé who had, by scaling the walls, stolen into the prison, as we have stated, knew to a minute what time each clock was to be "pegged," and the movements of the rescuing party were timed accordingly. Clock No. 1 having been duly "pegged" on this particular morning, and the watchman started on his tour of inspection, the two men who were so anxiously watching his movements followed slowly and softly behind him. The cell of Mr. Stephens was examined, the locks and bars found to be all correct, the prisoner apparently sleeping, and the watchman passed by, satisfied with his inspection. Scarcely had the sound of his footstep died out from within that cell, when it was approached by the two nameless individuals. Quickly the skeleton-key was applied to the lock, the bolts flew back, the barred door swung open, and "the captain," a moment since seemingly so sound asleep, stepped forth from the dismal cell and silently pressed the hands of his rescuers. But their work was not yet complete—barely commenced, in fact. In half an hour the watchman will return to clock No. 1, and again commence "pegging" his rounds, and "the captain" must be beyond his reach before that time. Hastily the two mysterious persons, accompanied by their chief, retraced their steps to where they had entered. Between the prison and the prison-garden there is a stone wall nearly twenty feet high. From the top of this dangled a rope-ladder; to mount this, and gain the summit of the wall, was but a moment's work. The rope-ladder was drawn up and lowered on the other side, and in another moment the three men had reached the prison-garden. Crossing this hastily, they approached another stone wall nearly as high as the one just scaled. The rope-ladder was once more brought into requisition, the top of the wall speedily gained, and at two o'clock and thirty-five minutes by the prison-clock, Mr. Stephens looked out upon the streets of Dublin. His friends outside were watching for him, and as they saw his form on the top of the wall, these devoted individuals closed in together, bending their backs for him to drop upon. Lightly he sprang down, landing safely and uninjured upon their shoulders, and he, for whose capture the British Government had made such prodigious efforts, stood upon his native soil once more a free man. His friends who had unlocked the door of his cell, having removed all traces of their flight, and having taken slight measures to mislead the authorities as to their mode of exit, hastily followed the example of their leader. No sooner had they landed than they immediately fled in different directions, Colonel Kelly and one other alone remaining with Mr. Stephens. The three walked rapidly for a few squares, when the third person was sent away; a few moments more and Mr. Stephens entered the house of a watching friend, and Colonel Kelly passed on to his lodgings. Both were drenched to the skin, splashed with mud, and their clothes bore evidence of the rough work they had encountered in scaling the prison-walls.

Six persons in different parts of the city and its

suburbs had been led to expect Mr. Stephens that night; all six kept their houses open awaiting his arrival, and had made every preparation to receive him. Colonel Kelly had anticipated every emergency which could arise, and had one mode of escape failed, another was open to him. Even had he been captured in the undertaking, his chief would still have escaped, and would have found his friends awaiting his arrival. The whole affair was most successfully managed, not one person about the prison being aware that the conspirator's cell was empty until four o'clock the following morning, unless, indeed, that official who furnished the impressions from which the skeleton keys were made, saw, in his dreams, the successful issue of the work to which he had contributed so much. Had any difficulty presented itself in the way of Mr. Stephens' escape that night, blood would doubtless have been shed. His friends did not encounter the danger of entering Richmond Prison without being prepared to force their way out, and each one, including Mr. Stephens, was well armed. Any person who would have ventured to oppose them would have been speedily put out of the way. If help had been needed, help was at hand. Eight thousand men were that night assembled at different points within the limits of the city of Dublin, ready to answer any call that might be made upon them by those whom they recognised as their leaders. Had there been any disturbance at the prison, that call would have been made, and these eight thousand men, ignorant of the reason why they were waiting, but knowing full well that some movement in the cause of Irish liberty was being made, would have made an onslaught upon Richmond Prison which would have reduced it to ruins. But, fortunately, this was not necessary. The daring revolutionary spirit had escaped from its walls, and was then as free as any Irishman in Ireland.

Mr. Stephens remained quietly at the house of the friend with whom he first lodged after leaving prison for over two weeks, and could, from his chamber-window, look out upon two sides of those stone walls which had, for thirteen days, shut him out from the world. Great was the hue and cry set up when his escape became known; again were the energies of the government bent upon his capture. The reward of £200 previously offered for his apprehension was increased to nearly £2,000, and numerous small rewards were offered by individuals. Mr. Stephens looked laughingly on while the detectives were stumbling by his hiding-place, and he frequently ventured forth into the streets of an evening and enjoyed his quiet walk and a cigar. He received the leading men of the Fenian organization occasionally at his rooms, and communicated with them all. Colonel Kelly, to whose skill and daring his escape was due, was the trusted Lieutenant of Mr. Stephens, and through him the business connected with the organization was mainly transacted. The Colonel occupied a suite of apartments in the busy part of the city, frequently met the Fenian leaders there, and yet was never even suspected by the vigilant police. With the exception of one night, Mr. Stephens did not sleep outside the limits of the city of Dublin from the time of his escape from prison until the

13th of March following, at which time he left Ireland for Paris on his way to America.

It was with feelings of the deepest regret that Mr. Stephens resolved to make the trip to America. The organization at home sadly needed his entire attention. The excitement consequent upon the arrests of Fenians, which were still being made by the government, was intense, and the British officials were congratulating themselves that dismay had seized upon and annihilated the Brotherhood. That a deep gloom had fallen upon the revolutionists was true; they had seen their companions dragged to prison by hundreds upon a bare suspicion, and the myrmidons of the oppressor were still at work; but disheartened or dismayed they were not. The spirit was ripe, and the determination for revolution more fixed than ever. Yet it needed the cool head and clear intellect of the Chief Organizer to steer the organization clear of all breakers. But the success of future movements depended upon the union of the opposing factions in America, and he believed that he could accomplish this.

THE AMERICAN TROUBLES.

The history of the unfortunate complications in American Fenian affairs, may be thus briefly summed up:

Colonel O'Mahony, the President of the organization, by persistently refusing to countenance any attempt at an invasion of Canada, had become quite unpopular. The Central Council had, despite the protest of Colonel O'Mahony, called a convention of State delegates, at which convention a Fenian Constitution was adopted. This document provided for a Senate, a War Department, a State Department, a Financial Department, and all the machinery of a Republican Government, and virtually robbed the President of a large portion of that power which had heretofore been vested in him. His hold upon the Brotherhood now rested almost solely upon the fact that his course was approved by Mr. Stephens and the Irish organization. The arrest of Mr. Stephens, it was believed, would not only prove his death-blow, but would also destroy Colonel O'Mahony's influence. The bonds of the Irish Republic were in process of printing, and the individual who had been selected as their custodian, had sent his signature to the engraver that a fac-simile of it might be made. The Senate finally objected to the issuing of the bonds, and their custodian refused to attach to them his signature. Knowing how much the cause at home was dependent on prompt action in America, Colonel O'Mahony had decided upon signing the bonds himself, and putting them in the market. The Senate took offence at this, and a session being called, a stormy debate ensued, at the conclusion of which Colonel O'Mahony was voted out of office, and Colonel Wm. R. Roberts chosen as his successor. But Colonel O'Mahony was not to be ousted so easily; he had many personal friends, and still more believed that his policy of sending assistance to the men at home was preferable to the Canadian scheme. These adhered to his fortunes, and he found himself still at the head of a powerful party. Party spirit ran high, and for a long time the press of the country teemed with the sayings and doings of the two factions.

FENIAN BROTHERHOOD.   85

This invasion of British dominions in America, and the seizure of certain towns from which large ships could be dispatched to all ports of the world through the rapid waters of the broad St. Lawrence river, had long been a favorite scheme of one party; and, though bitterly opposed by the other, its advocates had never ceased to urge it earnestly at all times and all places, in season and out of season. There were some other minor points discussed between the Fenian leaders, but the original cause of the breach in the ranks does not seem to have been anything more than a mere difference of opinion between some of the leaders as to the manner in which the campaign which is to break the British yoke was to be inaugurated. That a blow was to be struck at once was a point already decided on and agreed to by all the prominent men in the inmost or directing Circle of the Brotherhood. The disputed point was, "Where was England's most vulnerable, and at the same time, most accessible point? Would it be feasible to fight the first battle on Irish soil, thus literally bearding the lion in his den, or would it be advisable to adopt the plan of first securing a foothold somewhere on the American Continent from whence to deliver the first blow, in the coming combat?" In behalf of the latter plan, it was urged that it would be comparatively easy to seize upon some portion of the Canadian shore by a sudden raid, possess themselves of the principal Canadian towns, and thus, by a bold stroke, prove to the world that their claims to be considered among the " powers " were not wholly absurd, and their hopes of ultimate success not entirely chimerical. By this proceeding, it was argued, they would at once possess themselves of large quantities of much needed war material, and secure sites for military and naval dépôts, where they could assemble and organize their forces; through the great St. Lawrence river they could dispatch their ships, laden with troops and munitions of war. This undertaking, if successful, would give them a claim upon the nations to be accorded the rights of legitimate belligerents, and not to be regarded as a mere revolutionary horde, and to be treated as pirates if captured while engaged in destroying or damaging English commerce on the high seas. It was urged that it would be useless to attempt to throw a heavy force of soldiers into Ireland, except by the means of large and thoroughly equipped men-of-war which should be amply able to fight their way in case of being attacked by British cruisers. The possession of the large towns on the St. Lawrence would give them the opportunity to man and load the large ships which they proposed to purchase.

The opponents of this scheme objected to it, not so much that it seemed unlikely to succeed, as that it would almost of necessity involve a breach of the neutrality laws, and so invite the immediate and peremptory interference of the United States. It was also said, that the money of the organization had been given by the donors to be used on Irish soil, in aid of the struggling patriots on the Green Isle itself, and that to use it in any other way would be a perversion of the fund from its legitimate objects, and an inexcusable breach of good faith with the generous Irish sympathizers in this country, by whom every dollar had been given; and that it would also be a death-blow to the eager hopes of the "Men in the Gap," who have been so often and so positively promised aid from America, without which all their plans must fail, and all their sacrifices count as nothing.

Many and anxious were the discussions of the two plans by the Fenian leaders; but argument, instead of convincing, seemed only to aggravate differences, to engender personal animosities, and to stir up "Envy, hatred, malice, and all uncharitableness."

Time brought no healing on his wings, but day by day the strife grew more bitter. The advocates of the Canadian invasion, headed by Mr. Wm. R. Roberts and General Thomas W. Sweeny (who had served with distinction in the Union armies, during the Slaveholders' Rebellion), would not yield their point; and the other party, under the influence of O'Mahony, as positively refused to adopt the policy of their opponents.

Despite the discouragement of the O'Mahony wing, the Roberts men proceeded actively in their operations, and bought a large quantity of guns and other war-stores, enlisted their men, and, having decided on their objective point in Canada, all things were soon declared to be nearly in readiness.

Perceiving that the Roberts men were resolved on their Canadian attempt, Mr. O'Mahony finally yielded to a plan of Mr. B. Doran Killian's, which that gentleman had persistently and forcibly urged for some time. This was to organize a movement on Canada in opposition to the Roberts' raid, and by hurrying their own men first to that ground, to thus foil Roberts with his own weapons. They would thus earn for themselves all the *éclat* that was to be gained by being the first to inaugurate Fenian hostilities, and also to strike a bold blow at the hated Lion of England in his own dominions. Though his better judgment never approved the plan, at the last moment O'Mahony gave a most reluctant consent, and the movement was begun.

It is not our province, in this little book, to relate in detail the features of that lamentable Campo Bello *fiasco*. Suffice it to say, that it was a most ludicrous failure in every point. The whole plan, from its earliest inception to its ridiculous termination, seemed to be known in advance to the British authorities, who took measures to countercheck any move which could be made.

Discouraged, disheartened, sick, sore, sad, and sorry, the discomfited Fenians dispersed, and, with millions of hearty curses upon all connected with the management, or *mis*management of the affair, they slowly found their way back to their respective homes.

Of course the breach was now wider than ever, and the bitter recriminations of one party provoked retorts quite as savage and severe.

During the early progress of the Campo Bello scheme, while, in fact, it was in its infancy, a grand meeting of delegates convened from the Circles which remained true to the O'Mahony interest, and in a rapid but exceedingly busy session, they, with wonderful unanimity, expelled O'Mahony from his office as Head Centre of the Fenian Organization. Killian was also similarly expelled, and both were notified to turn over their books, documents, and funds, to a committee that had been appointed to take charge of them, and who were to manage the affairs of the Brotherhood until the arrival of Stephens, who was soon expected.

Meantime, the Roberts party, with their "Senate" and their Secretaries of War and the Navy, etc., still kept on as before, with much talk of mighty warlike preparations being made in secret.

This was the condition of affairs at the time of the advent of the great Chief Organizer on the 10th of May, 1866. The breach he was expected to heal seemed too wide to be spanned, but the Chief Organizer went manfully about the difficult task. How he succeeded Time alone can show, for as yet the problem is unsolved.

* * * * * * *

ADVENTURES OF STEPHENS ON HIS WAY TO THE UNITED STATES.

To set about this great work, it was necessary for Mr. Stephens to come to America. And accordingly, on the 11th of March, he left Dublin in company with Colonel Kelly and proceeded to a small harbor on the coast, where arrangements had been made to have a schooner in waiting to convey him to France. But a storm coming up prevented the schooner entering the harbor, and the two conspirators were compelled to remain over night. In the morning, a British revenue cutter came into the port, and all hope of getting aboard the schooner was destroyed. The two then returned to Dublin and made other arrangements. On the following day, Mr. Stephens drove through the streets of Dublin in an open carriage, alighted at one of the docks, and going on board a small schooner, was soon floating with the tide out of the harbor to the English Channel. Colonel Kelly was again his companion. Entering the Channel, they encountered head winds and stormy weather; were driven out of their course many miles, and finally were forced to put into Carrickfergus Bay. Again, they essayed to cross the Channel, and again encountered head winds and rough weather, but finally succeeded in making the little town of Ardrossan in Scotland. Here a car was procured which conveyed them to a neighboring railway station, where they took the train to London. Neither was disguised in any manner, and the entire journey was made openly without any attempt at concealment. That night, on their arrival in London, the Chief of the Irish Conspiracy and his Lieutenant slept at the Palace Hotel, directly opposite Buckingham Palace. The passage through England was made on St. Patrick's Day, the eighth anniversary of the Fenian Conspiracy. The English newspapers at this time were in the midst of a panic created by the rumors which reached them from the manufacturing districts. In these districts Fenianism was wide-spread among the workmen, and they had threatened that, in case England pursued towards the Fenians in Ireland the policy she had threatened, they would retaliate by burning all the manufacturing towns and destroying English property wherever found. At this time, Sir Hugh Rose, known as "The Butcher of India," was the commandant of Her Majesty's forces in Ireland, and had sought authority to pursue towards the Fenians the same course he had adopted with the rebel Sepoys in India, viz. blow them from the mouths of his cannon, roast them alive, etc., etc. The Irish in England indicated their determination to retaliate on English soil in case any such horrible outrages were perpetrated upon their brother-Irishmen at home. The country press was justly alarmed, and great excitement prevailed in consequence. Having rested themselves sufficiently, Mr. Stephens and Colonel Kelly took the train to Dover, thence to Calais, and, on the night of the 18th of April, relieved of all thought of danger, and beyond the reach of their persecutors, they slept peacefully in Paris.

Mr. Stephens, while in Paris, was cordially received by many prominent French noblemen and politicians, among whom was the Marquis de Boissy. At his house the Irish revolutionist ate and drank, receiving from his kind host words of sympathy and encouragement. While in Paris, Mr. Stephens was joined by his wife, and having provided for her a proper residence in which to remain during his American visit, he was prepared to leave the land in which he had, for the third time, found so many friends in the hour of his trouble.

ARRIVAL OF MR. STEPHENS IN NEW YORK.—ENTHUSIASM OF THE FENIANS.

On the 28th day of March he embarked from Havre in the steamship Napoleon III., and, after a voyage of thirteen days, the " Central Organizer of the Irish Republic" arrived in New York on the evening of Thursday, May 10, 1866. His arrival had been expected for several days, and the two or three hours' notice given by the outlying telegraph at Sandy Hook, was amply sufficient for the gathering of a large and most enthusiastic crowd which assembled about the dock where the French steamer was to land her passengers.

Would it be well to attempt to describe the feeling among the Fenians? We think not. A more excited set of men and women was never known. A Committee from the Moffat mansion had been appointed to receive the distinguised Conspirator, and were anxiously awaiting him at the dock. Mr. Stephens was first seen and recognised by the Committee as the ship was swinging her stern into the slip, and when recognised he was cheered vociferously by the Committeemen and others who had been admitted within the gates. These plaudits assured the great multitude outside and on neighboring wharves that the chief of the Fenians was really about to step on American soil, and they took up the cheers and threw their hats high in air in unbounded enthusiasm. The news of the distinguised arrival had been communicated to the shipping in the harbor, and the passing steamers blew a deafening welcome, while a piece of Fenian artillery on the New Jersey shore thundered forth a national salute. The masses of human beings on West street and on the wharves— and particularly outside the gates of Pier No. 50— became denser and denser as the minutes flew on, and the number of privileged persons who were permitted to pass the gates grew apace, until the ship was ready to take aboard her gang-plank. At this moment the pressure towards the ship's gangway was not only decidedly uncomfortable but really perilous; a platoon of policemen soon cleared the required space, and when the gang-plank had been properly adjusted, the distinguished guest of the Committee appeared, leaning on the arm of Colonel Kelly. A deafening huzza went up, and in another moment the Fenian Chief was in the midst of his Irish-American friends. A brief consultation ensued, and Mr. Stephens and staff, consisting of Capt. M. E. O'Brien, of Keokuk, Iowa; Lieut. William Smith O'Brien, of Detroit; Lieut. James M. Gibbons, of New York, and Chief-Engineer Thomas Moore, were conducted to the coaches in waiting.

The impetuosity of a Celtic-American crowd is proverbial. The one which gathered on the wharves and in the streets that day was particularly so; and the wild and enthusiastic Fenians, in their unbridled love for their chief, came near killing him with kindness before they had fairly made his acquaintance.

Outside the gates the crush was fearful. It was with extreme difficulty that the Committee were able to get Mr. Stephens and staff safely into their carriages and off the pier; and it is indeed matter of wonder that of the multitudes who climbed upon the vehicles, and almost fell under the horses' feet in endeavoring to get their hands through the coach windows and into those of Stephens, not one was the victim of any accident.

The coaches were driven off at a moderate trot up Barrow-street, with a noisy multitude bringing up the rear and on the sides of the street; and this crowd rapidly augmented until, on the arrival of the party at the Metropolitan Hotel, it filled Broadway from curb to curb.

In the course of the many interviews which Mr. Stephens held with his friends and admirers that evening, though they were, from the nature of the circumstances, short and hurried, he assured his friends that he had not even dreamed of making the transit of the Atlantic until long after the disastrous division occurred in the Fenian organization here, and he should not even now have come had not many warm friends urged him to visit America with a view to harmonizing the Fenian Order. He had come to conciliate and to win, if possible, every true Irishman over to one common Centre, through whom the great work of liberating Ireland may yet be made an accomplished fact. The people of Ireland were ripe for the shock of war in September last, and he had no doubt that Ireland might have now been one of the sovereign nations of the earth had it not been for the rupture of the organization here. But even if the nation's independence could not have been achieved in so short a time, certainly the power of the British army in Ireland could have been broken, and by this time England would have lost her foothold everywhere except on the coast and in the seaboard cities. But he said the work may yet be wrought out if Irishmen in America will make a united effort. He was willing that bygones should be bygones, and that all past acrimonious speeches might be now forgotten, and all private animosities merged in the one desire to place the cause of Ireland on a sure and hopeful footing. For his own part, he promised to throw himself unreservedly into any measure which should promise to hasten that great and glorious future which he so fondly anticipates for his native land, no matter by whom such a scheme or plan should be originated.

PERSONAL APPEARANCE OF MR. STEPHENS.

The personal appearance of Mr. Stephens made a decidedly favorable impression upon the many friends who called to see him at his hotel. He is a thick-set, wiry-looking man, about five feet three or four inches tall, and dresses in a plain, simple business suit. His head is quite bald, revealing a bold, prominent forehead. What hair he has is of a light color, wavy in appearance, and very fine. His complexion is florid, his eye keen and penetrating. The expression of his face is mild, and, when lighted up with smiles, his eyes beaming with mirth, is very pleasant to look upon. His manners are exceedingly affable and agreeable, and his language betokens the true Irish gentleman. The words which flow from his mouth are tinged with that "sweet Irish brogue" which is so pleasant to hear when spoken by persons of cultivation.

The subjoined "Phrenological Description" of Mr. Stephens is so good and true that it is worthy of being copied :

"His is the face of a man who is confessedly the most accomplished 'conspirator,' or organizer of conspiracy, Ireland has seen since the days of the gallant and self-devoted Theobald Wolfe Tone. But I see no resemblance between the two men. In the portrait of Tone you have a delicate, slender face, which would be almost womanish but for the firm chin, the nervous-breathing nostril, and the quick-glancing, brilliant eye. This is a comely face, too, but of a different order. Tone's was fiery, soldierly; the prevailing expression here, at first sight, is unqualified *bonhomie*—the unruffled good-humor of a man who is content with himself and all the world beside.

"Look a little more closely at this face. Meeting its owner in the street, in this bearded age, you would pass him by as a respectable citizen in the prime of life (engaged in commerce, perhaps), the placid serenity of whose mind was not disturbed by even the thought of a bill of exchange to be met on the fourth of the month. There is a quiet smile on the mouth and a cheerful gleam, a very amusing twinkle of dry humor in the eyes—no more. Surely thousands who have seen this portrait must have felt sadly disappointed. The general English mind pictured the original as a modern Guy Fawkes: a dark, frowning villain, who lurked in hidden places, and went abroad at night, with revolvers in his bosom and a dagger in his sleeve—a keen-eyed, hook-nosed, thin-lipped, slouching fellow, who would as soon blow the Lord-lieutenant, and the privy council, and the bishops to boot into eternity, as bless himself. What a disappointment to those who conjured up such a picture, this placid, good-humored, self-contented face must be.

"But look again. The face of a fair-haired man this is, with bald temples and flowing beard. The forehead is unusually massive, but so rounded and dome-like in shape as to have that massiveness much softened down. What the phrenologists would call the organs of benevolence and ideality are very large. The perceptive organs are remarkably well developed, as are those of locality and time; and I have never seen what is called the organ of individuality more largely developed, except in one or two great actors. If there be the least shadow of truth in the so-called science of phrenology, the owner of this face must be a marvellous reader of character. This is what is called a 'well-bred' face; the expression is decidedly gentlemanly, and you could not possibly conceive the original being obtrusive or self-asserting in general company; on the contrary, I should set him down as a retiring person. But clear through all this outward show, as through a filmy veil, comes another and a deeper expression—the inner man. I read absolute and unbounded self-reliance; firm, calm, indomitable, iron will; unqualified belief in a cause, and unshaken confidence in its ultimate success in spite of every disaster. Here is the face of a man whom no defeat conquers; stopped and baulked on one path without fretting or chafing, he calmly turns to another, and marches on. With a massive brain, (and so equally balanced a brain I have, perhaps, never seen, as this portrait seems to indicate), teeming with inexhaustible resources, he flings away his failing scheme, without a moment's hesitation, to grasp at a new one, and runs the whole scale of plot and contrivance with the ease of an artist at his piano.

"No failure can daunt such a man; with such a man, to cease to strive is to cease to live. This all-abounding faith in himself and his cause, and inexhaustible fertility of resources, would buoy him up amid the billows of an ocean of disasters. But there is another characteristic of which mention should not be omitted. This portrait indicates a man singularly gifted with the power of winning the affection and confidence of others. It is not that graceful *bonhomie*, that hearty manner, that genial smile (which, by the way, cannot overmaster the keen, clear, piercing glance of the eye), which helped him alone in this; it is, that the magnetic power of his own unbounded faith inspires like faith in the breasts of others. In conclusion, this is the face of a man of great vital power and intense nervous energy. The blending of oak-like firmness and velvet softness which I read in this fine head and face is very singular; it recalls the old idea of the iron hand in the velvet glove. This head is a noble specimen of the Southern Irish type, which I have already pointed out. But, talking of hands, have you ever noted how a man's hand serves as an index of character? In the portrait before me, the arms are folded, and the left hand rests on the right arm. It is soft and white, with long tapering prehensile fingers. A very significant hand, that, not so much expressive of power as of undying tenacity of purpose. At the foot of the portrait, I read the name—JAMES STEPHENS."

A SERENADE.—RESIGNATION OF HEAD CENTRE JOHN O'MAHONY.

On the evening following the arrival of Mr. Stephens in New York, he was serenaded at his hotel. A dense crowd collected in the street, completely blocking it up from curb to curb for the distance of an entire square. At eleven o'clock, Mr. Stephens appeared upon the balcony of the hotel, his presence being greeted by the crowd with tremendous cheers, flinging up of hats, etc. He thanked them kindly for the honor done him, but declined making a lengthy speech until such time as he should have made himself more familiar with the existing troubles among his countrymen in America. The enthusiastic multitude would scarcely permit him to retire, insisting upon being allowed the privilege of looking at him though he said not a word. Upon being assured that he would address them at a future day, he was allowed to return to his rooms.

The first official act performed by Mr. Stephens after his arrival in New York was the acceptance of the resignation of Colonel John O'Mahony as Head Centre of the Fenian Brotherhood. The following correspondence, in reference to this patriotic move on the part of Colonel O'Mahony, explains the motives which prompted him to such action:

HEADQUARTERS F. B.,
NEW YORK, *May* 11, 1866.

James Stephens, C. E. F. B.:

BROTHER: I feel it to be imperatively incumbent upon me, at this momentous crisis in Irish affairs, to tender you my resignation as the Head Centre of the Fenian Brotherhood and Agent of the Irish Republic.

My reasons for this step are twofold. The first is my consciousness of the fact that in consenting to the recent disastrous attempt to capture Campo Bello, I violated my duty, not alone to the Fenian Brotherhood and the Irish Republic, but to the best interests of the Irish race, as also to my previous unvaried policy. It matters little now to recapitulate what were the arguments and what the pressure brought to bear upon me in order to force me to depart from my settled plan of action. Enough that the attempt has ended in disaster—that the energies of the Brotherhood have been paralysed, and that, unless you can restore it to hope and vigor, its object will have been defeated and its long years of hopeful trial will have ended in a fiasco.

My second reason for resigning arises from a hope that I shall thereby remove an obstacle to union upon a common Irish platform, under your guidance, among all of my countrymen that are true and sincere in the cause of our native land. Mixed up as I have been in the recent quarrels among the American Fenians, many good Irishmen may regard me with feelings of personal hostility with which they cannot now regard you.

Trusting that your advent to America, at the present juncture, may be productive of all the good to our race that the Fenian Brotherhood and myself expect of it, and that it may promote unity of plan and concert of action, fraternal harmony with stedfast hope and firm resolve in the Fenian ranks, I have the honor to remain in fraternity,

Your obedient servant,
JOHN O'MAHONY, H. C. F. B.

Mr. Stephens' acceptance of the resignation is couched in the following language:

METROPOLITAN HOTEL, NEW YORK, *May* 11, 1866.
To John O'Mahony, Esq.:

BROTHER: In my opinion you have acted wisely and patriotically in tendering your resignation under actual circumstances. No man worth that name questions your honor and devotion to Ireland. But the united action we desire so much, and to effect which I left Ireland, at your invitation, would be impossible while you directed affairs here. It must be needless to tell you why. I feel bound, however, to say that, in sanctioning the late most deplorable divergence from the true path, you not only gave proof of weakness, but committed a crime less excusable in you than any other man. For you should have known that your project, however successful, would have resulted in our ruin. And you should have recollected how I supported you in a critical moment, because I believed you were opposed to every project that would lead the true Irishmen of this continent from the original aim and holiest duty of the Fenian Brotherhood—direct assistance to the 'men in the gap.' Everything considered then, I feel imperatively called on to accept your resignation. But while accepting it I still rely upon your hearty coöperation, as I now rely on the coöperation of every true man of our race.

Convinced that the Irish *people* are with me everywhere, I have not a doubt of being able to accomplish what I came for; and so, in good cheer, and unswerving faith, I am yours, fraternally,

JAMES STEPHENS, C. O. I. R.

This act of Colonel O'Mahony was considered by the members of the Brotherhood as an unselfish and purely patriotic proceeding, and gave universal satisfaction. It was hoped and believed that the example would be followed by the leader of the other Fenian wing, and that Colonel Roberts would at once proffer his resignation.

But this was not to be. The Senate would not listen to the proposition, that body having become too fully committed to the Canadian invasion policy to permit them to recede. In justice to Mr. Roberts, however, it should be stated that he expressed his earnest wish to do whatever should be deemed best for his native country, and to unite the Brotherhood in America.

FENIAN MASS MEETING AT JONES' WOOD—SPEECH OF MR. STEPHENS.

The Fenian Brotherhood of New York, desiring to give Mr. Stephens a public reception, and also to affording him an opportunity of explaining to his countrymen the condition of affairs in their native land, resolved upon holding an open-air festival. Jones' Wood, a large park in the suburbs of the city, was the place selected for this demonstration, and Tuesday, May 15th, the time appointed. The time for preparation was short; and the notices of the meeting were not so generally circulated as they should have been. An admission fee of half a dollar was charged, the proceeds to be immediately turned over to Mr. Stephens for the benefit of the cause in Ireland. Despite these drawbacks, and the fact that the meeting was held on a week-day, when few mechanics could leave their workshops, a great crowd was present. Not less than 15,000 people contributed to the enthusiasm of the occasion.

A large number of Fenian Circles sent duly appointed delegates, most of whom were assigned to duty in the preservation of good order and the sale of tickets. Members of the following, among other circles, were present, bearing flags, banners, and mottoes, and marching to the sound of the ever popular and stirring music of dear old Erin. Hamilton Rowan Club, Brian Boru, Malachi, McHale, Renburg, Red Hand, Wolfe Tone Cadets, Davis, Fontenoy Cadets, Corcoran, Brother Sheares, Laville, Clontarf, O'Mahony, Tara, Faugh-a-ballagh, James Stephens, Garryowen, Long Island, Connaught Rangers, Sarsfield, Stephens, Hibernia, Wolf Tone, Rock of Cashel, O'Gorman, Killian, Geraldine, Clark Luby, Richard D. Williams, Hugh O'Neil, Garryowen Cadets, Michael Moore, St. Patrick, Irish People, Volunteers of 1782, Thomas Francis Meagher, O'Regan, General Kearney, McClellan, Gem of the Sea, Robert Emmet, Patrick Henry, Sarsfield Cadets, Owen Roe O'Neill, Napper Tandy, Lord Clare, Harp of Erin, Dungannon, Volunteers of 1782, Dalcette, Hope, Montgomery, Vinegar Hill, John O'Leary, O'Donnell-Aboo, St. Lawrence O'Toole, Cahir O'Doughty, Neptune, J. Barry, and United Irishmen.

Among those persons present in the Committee-room to receive the distinguished leader of the Irish people, were Major-General Joe Hooker and Brigadier-General Ruggles, of General Meade's staff; Judge Connolly and Denis J. Gaffney, of Albany, who studied law with Thomas Addis Emmet; Colonel P. J. Downing, John J. Marion, Centre, of Albany; Colonel Thomas Philip O'Reilly, of General Sherman's staff; Michael R. Kenney, State Centre, New Jersey; John McKenna, Troy, State Centre, New York; Jeremiah Kavanagh, California.

At half-past two o'clock an order was issued to those in the reception-room to fall in procession. When the movement commenced, all was smooth sailing till it came in contact with the crowd outside, when such a rush took place as displaced the guard who were clearing a passage. Mr. Stephens was hurried through a narrow space by a few members of the Committee, and though there was a continual pressure of the crowd in whatever point he advanced, he treated them in the style of his retreat from Richmond Prison. While some of his attendants were tugging with the crowd to save their coat-skirts, he was up the ladder and in his position on the platform. An indiscriminate throng, with overpowering force, swept policemen and guards aside and gained the summit. Efforts were made to stem the pressure, in which some luckless individuals were precipitated from their lofty eminence to the nether regions. Everything was now chaos, and the "hero of Richmond," proverbial for ingenuity and stratagem, executed a flank movement on the bewildered occupants of the platform. He descended, and without much difficulty took his stand on the small stage adjacent.

After order and silence were to some extent obtained, Mr. Stephens proceeded to address the assemblage as follows:

FRIENDS OF IRELAND.—Towards the close of December, 1857, a young Irishman called at my residence in Dublin, bringing me letters from Colonel O'Mahony and from the late Colonel Michael Doheny. He had also an oral communication to make himself; but all was to the effect that an organization had been established in America, of which Colonel Doheny was appointed the chief, and I was requested to commence an organization and to direct it in Ireland. At that time the cause of Ireland was so low at home as well as abroad—in fact, throughout the world—that few men of any brains or position could be got to take part in it. They did not know the people. The Irish people were then, as ever, sound. Their hearts were in the right place, and they only required to be shown what to do that they might do it. On my return to Ireland after seven years' exile, the first thing I did was to travel through the country in every direction to derive a thorough knowledge of the people, and to see what could be done. I devoted a whole year to that, during which time I travelled three thousand miles on foot. (A Voice—" Were you ever in Tipperary?" (Cheers.) Yes, often. There is not a spot from Slievenamon to Ballinderry that I don't know. (Great cheering.) You know the words of Thomas Davis,

> From Carrick-on-Suir to Galtamore,
> From Slievenamon to Ballinderry.   (Great cheering.)

You see I know it. With this knowledge of the people I conscientiously answered the letters of my friends in America, and on certain conditions I undertook to organize a force of ten thousand men in three months in Ireland. I undertook to do no more at that time. The conditions I exacted were twofold. First, that I should have absolute direction and control of the organization. I believe that you know this was a conspiracy, and a conspiracy in Ireland against British rule. And I believe it utterly impossible for any oppressed nationality to organize such a power as could effect its independence without a conspiracy, and without one man having the supreme control in that conspiracy. For that reason, and for that alone, in the interest of the movement I undertook to unite, I deemed it necessary to make that the first condition—that I should have supreme control of the organization. The second condition was that I should be supplied with certain sums of money per month. I asked for the small sum of from £80 to £100 a month for the first three months. After this time, having organized ten thousand men, I meant to have made other proposals. I sent a trusted friend, who has since been in an Irish prison, to America, on that occasion, with my answer. On the 17th March, 1858, he returned; he had found no organization in America, only a few devoted men, at the head of which was Mr. Doheny—(a voice—"Poor fellow, I knew him well!")—who had held together against all circumstances in America, and who were then endeavoring to keep the Irish feeling alive and make it a power there. But he found no organization. There was but this nucleus of twenty or thirty men. They accepted my conditions and sent me a paper endorsing, so far as they could endorse it, my action in Ireland. On the 17th of March, then, 1858, I began the organization in Ireland. As I told you, it was a conspiracy. To become a member of this conspiracy it was necessary to take an oath. You have heard a good deal on the subject of this oath, but perhaps you have not heard my real reason for making it an essential condition of membership. I had been in the movement in 1848 with Smith O'Brien, and we found when we had a hundred, or two or three hundred men around us, if we happened to meet in any place where the clergymen happened to be against the movement, they invariably spoke against it, and they were able to scatter our force, such as it was. This was because the people had not been trained; they had not got the necessary training, and it was necessary to get the people, in my mind, to distinguish between the twofold character of the priest—the clergymen of all classes—to distinguish between their temporal and spiritual character. We have invariably inculcated upon our friends the duty of giving obedience and submitting in all devotion to their clergy in their spiritual character, but that in their temporal character they were simply to look upon them as citizens. (Vociferous cheering.) Without this training you never could have a force in Ireland on whom you could reply. We then made the oath a condition of membership, and we have continued to make it so. It shall not be changed. (Cries of "Good.") The first instalment of the money sent to me from America (£90), I received on the 17th of March, 1858. The second instalment was to have reached me a month from that; but the months of April, May, and June, went by without my receiving anything. Then, the second time, I had to send out my trusted friend to America to state the case. The report he brought to New York was favorably received; but as there was no organization in America at the time, he found it very difficult to get the necessary funds. These came to me in small instalments. I continued to work, however, drawing on the resources of my friends at home in Ireland; for I want to make you understand that for every dollar contributed in this country, men at home have contributed ten. (Great cheering.) Finding, about the month of September, that the promise made to me remained unfulfilled, and knowing that I had organized more than ten times the force I had undertaken to organize, I felt the necessity of coming to America to lay the foundation of our work here. In September, 1858, I arrived in New York, and had a great many difficulties to contend with here. But of these difficulties I do not care to speak at length now, though, if necessary, I shall make them all known to you, but not now. I have too many other points to touch upon. At length, however, I was allowed to go to work in America, and the first man I enlisted in the organization, or one of the first, was General Corcoran. (Cheers.) At that time the organization in America was a secret society, as it was in Ireland. It has been found politic to change it in that regard since; it has been changed; but whether for the better or not the future can only tell. I travelled through the States and laid the foundation of this organization. On my return to New York a document was drawn up conferring upon me the supreme control of this organization, at home and abroad (cheers); in America as well as in Ireland and England, and in Australia—everywhere our race can be found—from that day out. It was only after a residence of from two to four months in the States I was allowed to go to work, and, as they were impatient for me to return to Ireland, I had only a month to devote to the work of organization in this city, and I had no time at all to collect any amount of funds or arms, or what we needed in Ireland; but all these things were

promised to me. However, they did not come. I believe this is
one of the points upon which you want information—the amount
of support we in Ireland have received from here from the beginning of the organization. Well, then, to be brief, during the
first six years of the organization in America, we in Ireland received from you about one thousand five hundred pounds. I have
come to America to establish harmony in this organization, and
woe to the man who says or does anything to prevent that.
(Great cheering.) Let there be no cries against Doran Killian or
John O'Mahony, against General Sweeny or Colonel Roberts; let
there be no cries here to-day against any man. If you have come
in a spirit of brotherhood, well; if not, woe to you and woe to Ireland. (Sensation.) Let every man who has come here to-day,
if such be here, for the purpose of creating dissension and discord
in our ranks—to widen the breach unhappily existing—let that
man go home from here—let him go home. (Cheering). This is
no place for him; let him go to England, that is the place for
him—(cheers)—let him go to the British Ambassador; there he
will be received; but let him not stand here with Irishmen who
have sworn to free their land or die. (Great cheering.) I, for
my single self, have had my troubles. I have been infinitely
more tried by my friends than by my foes; the men who used to
call themselves my friends and the friends of Ireland, have proved
deadlier enemies to Ireland and me than British tyranny could
ever do. But I must not anticipate. I speak to you in a spirit
of brotherhood. I want to have you united, I want to have all
our race come into the work, like brother Irishmen and patriots,
and any man or body of men who prevents union, I here, to-day,
in the face of you all, and in the name of Ireland, brand them as
traitors to Ireland and enemies to our race. (Tremendous cheering.) Our motto to-day shall be union. (Continued cheering.)
Each man among us must give up selfishness and shortsighted
opinions and come into the great brotherhood. You can all do
it. (Cheering.) You are the people, you are the power; you
can make the men, you can direct the men, you can force them
into the right way and prevent them going astray from it.
(Cheers.) The duty is upon you to-day, and you must do it.
(Cheers and cries of "We will.") To come back to my narrative
—for it is merely a narrative, and I mean it to be so, rather than
a speech—for the first six years after this organization, as I said,
we in Ireland received in all about £1,500. We were driven almost back upon our resources, and I am sorry that we did not
trust to our own resources alone—that we ever looked to America for anything whatever. For, from the spirit of dissension that
sprang up, the amount of calumny, misrepresentation, bad feeling,
bad blood and scandal that was indulged in in this organization,
shame was brought upon us all over the world, and it can only
be blotted out by the redemption of Ireland. (Cheers.) About
the year 1863 I found there remained to me three courses to pur-

sue. I had almost despaired of getting anything done from this side, and it seemed to me at home that we were bound to make another effort. We had then one of the best men the people knew in Ireland. I sent him out here with a statement of affairs. That man has since been condemned to twenty years' penal servitude; he is now a 'felon,' with felon's clothes, doing felon's work, obliged to associate with the assassin, the burglar, the scoundrel, with the scum of the earth, and placed by British law on the same level with those criminals. He was my trusted friend, a trusted Irishman in the cause of Ireland—learned, patriotic, and accomplished. He was of a trusting nature, and believed the representations made to him here in America. He wrote home in great heart to his friends, all of whom his letter cheered except myself. His letter brought no cheer to me, for from what I had already heard I knew his mission would be a failure. I knew that from his first letter to me. That was the first course open to me—to send this man to America upon the people's work. His mission was a failure. The next course open to me was to establish a newspaper in Ireland and get for it as wide a circulation as possible, and devote its proceeds to the organization. You must know that greater difficulties arise in raising money in Ireland than in this country. I will not give the poverty of the people as a reason for this. Poor as the people of Ireland are to-day, if I could have one month's tour there, as I could in these States, I would raise as much money as would free Ireland. But I was not free to move about Ireland. It was necessary for me, as head of this organization, to travel with caution, and it was because I did so I was able to escape from arrest so long. But in a short time I received sufficient money to establish the *Irish People*, of which you have heard a great deal. Towards the establishment of that paper I got no assistance whatever, as every obstacle was put in the way of its circulation, and it became dangerous for a seller to sell it, or a purchaser to buy it; for the government were watching the sale of the paper. The landlords and employers, having a large number of people as their dependents, brought their influence to bear, and I am sorry to add that the clergy set their faces against the paper, so that it was difficult to effect a large circulation. The Chicago Fair was announced, and shortly after, an Irishman who did good service in the cause of Ireland, was deputed to go from Chicago to Ireland to represent the state of affairs to us. Ostensibly he went to buy goods for the fair, and receive what we contributed; but in reality came and represented that nothing could save the organization from ruin but my presence in America, and the committee in Chicago were anxious that I should come, else the organization would fall to the ground. In this narrative I am omitting many details, because I wish to speak in a spirit of conciliation, and I do not wish to let one word fall from my lips to hurt any man. If any word of mine should hurt him by chance

I beg his pardon beforehand, and say that I did not mean it. I came to the States. The gentleman alluded to is Mr. Henry Clarence McCarty. I asked him, among other things, if the entire proceeds of the fair would be placed in my hands for service in the cause of Ireland, and on his representations and promises I came a second time to the States. I promised my friends in Ireland, on my arrival in New York, to send them £100; on my arrival in Chicago, another £100, and in a week after my arrival in Chicago, £1,000. The £100 was sent from New York, according to promise; then another £100, and £1,000 from Chicago. For a considerable time I could receive no more money. There was a State convention held in Chicago at that time, and Mr. O'Mahony attended it as well as the centres of the Western States. Mr. O'Mahony, on being called on to say what was the strength of the Fenian Brotherhood at that time in America, stated that he could not claim more than ten thousand in it. As my object in coming to the States was to collect money and receive arms in order to bring the movement to a close as soon as possible, I felt that with so small a basis I could not effect my purpose. I felt that in Chicago on that night, and I continued to feel it for eight or ten days as I went through the States—through towns of Illinois—and it was only when I got to St. Louis that I began to see my way, and felt that if put in proper working order the organization would realize all my expectations in a short time. And here I may say, that we never required much. Those people who told you that I came over for two hundred thousand, or fifty thousand, or twenty thousand men, or one-half that number, knew very little about me, and still less about Ireland. (Cheers.) At that time we would have been perfectly satisfied with a few men. All we then wanted was war material. On my return to New York, I had certain changes to propose, which were, in my opinion essential to success First, I deemed it necessary that Mr. O'Mahony should have a deputy Head Centre, an able business man, who could make good certain defects in Mr. O'Mahony, for Mr. O'Mahony was always opposed to making direct appeals for money, and it was absolutely necessary that these appeals should be made. He was also not disposed to go to strange parts of this continent when invitations were not forthcoming. The invitations did not come. Certain other changes I deemed necessary, and these changes effected an extraordinary improvement, which very soon became visible in the organization. That which had real effect on the people of this continent was, I believe, the statement I made to them in 1864. That statement was to the effect that the organized force at that time in Ireland was sixty thousand men, just six times the strength of your legal, open organization in America; and I made the engagement that if England went to war that year on the Danish question, we should take the field, but that whether England went to war or not, we should take the field in 1865.

What the people wanted here as well as in Ireland was a fixed time for action, and not to be dragged on, as they had been for years, without knowing when the time for action would come. To the statement then made, much of the progress made is to be attributed. On my return to Ireland I found that the work was in a very good state, and the report that I brought back from America set the people at work still harder. But still the war did not take place. England fought shy, as she has often since the establishment of our organization. She did not go to war on the Danish question, and we had then one year more to wait. You held your Cincinnati convention, and about that time I wrote, stating the requirements of Ireland, and asking for the months of January, February, and March, £1,000. I stated I would require for the month of April, £1,000 alone, and for the months of May, June, July, and August, about £2,500 per month. The money for January, February, and March was sent to me—about £1,000. Another £1,000 was sent to me in April, but I did not get the second instalment till the middle of May, and of the money for May, June, July, and August, I got none. Instead of getting the money I asked for, and which would have enabled us to take the field last year, two gentlemen were appointed here to go to Ireland to investigate our work. They were perfectly satisfied with the state of affairs in Ireland. They sent over a very favorable report, and asked for money to be sent back to us. It was agreed on at that time that the bonds of the Irish republic should be issued upon their return. It was calculated we should have all that was requisite by the close of the year. It so happened that one of the delegates, while in Ireland, lost certain documents. This was Mr. Meehan. (There was some hissing when Mr. Meehan's name was mentioned.) Now, I don't wish to say one word disparagingly of him to-day; neither do I wish that any friend of mine should do so; but while desirous of not saying anything against him, it is necessary that the fact should be known that the loss of these documents was the immediate occasion of the arrests in Ireland. (Groaning.) I have myself written against him, and if I have wronged him I would be very happy to make ample reparation if he will only favor me with a visit. (Cheers.) I have sent invitations to all those gentlemen—General Sweeny, Mr. Roberts and Mr. Meehan—to all of those gentlemen to come and see me; but very few of them have come, I am sorry to say. The fault, however, has not been mine. I have made all the advances compatible with my sense of duty and of dignity. Well, the arrests were made, and the government said triumphantly that all was over in Ireland. But so far from it, never was harder work and more work done in Ireland than immediately after the arrests. I was free myself, and while free I am not used to be idle. (Great cheering.) Immediately afterwards, the government saw the necessity of proclaiming every county in Ireland, one after the other, because they felt that the work was going on stronger than ever, and that the only thing we wanted was arms and munitions of war, and these were coming into the country, and they could not prevent their coming in. They saw that the men who were serving the cause of Ireland were able to baffle them, and that the men got in what they required. What they were able to do then, they are able to do now. Don't allow yourselves to be blinded upon that subject, nor let yourselves be persuaded by any one that we can't get the means into the country. It has been all a question of money With the requisite funds we can get in whatever materials we wish, and men too, if we require them. My opinion on this subject ought to be more than the opinions of the people who have not seen Ireland since the greenness of their youth, and who know next to nothing of Ireland. (Cheers.) My friends were arrested, and you know how they conducted themselves. The bearing of those prisoners has not been surpassed by the bearing of any men in history, under similar circumstances. And they bore all this because they still had faith—faith in the organization which they knew to be so powerful at home, and also faith that the promises so often made to them, and so solemnly made upon this side, would be kept. When the counties had been proclaimed, the British press—and how am I to designate that press?—I believe it to be the vilest in the world, unless it be that foul press of Ireland, which may fairly be designated the journalistic excrements of England—that vile press then began to boast that the organization was suppressed in Ireland. But only a few weeks afterwards the Lord Lieutenant wrote the precious letter which you must have all read, calling on the government to suspend the Habeas Corpus Act. You know the wholesale arrests that were made after the suspension of the Habeas Corpus. They thought to make the world believe that we were suppressed then at least, and that was their third attempt. But I can tell you now that the organization in Ireland to-day is stronger than it ever had been, in numbers, discipline, and in all the requirements of an army, save only in war material. The organization in Ireland, towards the close of last year, numbered two hundred thousand men, and of that force, fifty thousand were thoroughly drilled, with a large proportion of men who had seen war and smelt powder on the battlefield—a large proportion of veterans, in short; fifty thousand were partly drilled men, and the other hundred thousand quite undrilled. But if there be a man among you who thinks that fifty thousand Irishmen thoroughly drilled, with fifty thousand others partly drilled, would not make a force sufficient to meet anything that England could bring against us, then indeed he is wofully ignorant of the resources of England. What army could be brought against Ireland by England? What is the military force of England at present? There are some twenty thousand

English troops in Ireland at present, and it would take England from thirty to forty days to concentrate a force of thirty or forty thousand men in Ireland. It would take her three months at least to concentrate a force of seventy thousand, and it is not likely she would be ever able to concentrate a larger force. Of our forces we could concentrate in Ireland, at four or five given points, one hundred thousand men in twenty-four hours. (Tremendous cheering.) All we wanted in Ireland from the middle of September to the end of December was arms to put into the hands of our men. The men were there, and only wanted the arms. But, in the very hour of our strength, there came to Ireland the melancholy news of your disruption here. Still we held on. We did not think it possible that any body of men on this continent could be found that would withhold from Ireland in that supreme hour of her need the succor which they had promised to give us; and it was because I could not bring myself to believe this that I had made up my mind to get myself arrested, even if the English authorities had not succeeded in doing so; for I felt myself bound to action last year, and I thought you would feel bound to it here, if I devoted myself so far as to accept a prison voluntarily, and that by going into prison you on this side would be driven to give us what we wanted. However, before the time I had decided for putting it into execution I heard nothing favorable from this side, and the government found out my residence and I was arrested. I suppose you would all like to know how I got out of prison. (Tremendous enthusiasm.) Well, it did not require any extraordinary effort on my part, for with the force of true hearts that were around that prison in Dublin it would not have been possible for the government, though the walls had been of adamant, and though it had regiments stationed within those walls, to keep me there. (Great cheering.) To my friends in Dublin, then, I refer you for the manner in which I effected my escape. That was the time of our greatest power in Ireland, and if, at any time between the 24th of November and the end of December, you had sent to Ireland a small force, or only a few superior officers with the necessary war material, I do believe, as firmly as in my own existence, that Ireland would be an independent country to-day. But you know what took place. However, my mind was made up not to leave Ireland, and so I remained for nearly four months in Dublin city after my escape from prison. At length I had an invitation from Mr. O'Mahony and others to come to this country, for the organization, it was said, required my presence here.

The evening after the reception of this invitation, I called some of my most trusted friends around me to hold a council, to see, before I determined on starting for America, if something might not be done at home even without your assistance. It was dedermined on that night, even without asking for my voice, to defer action yet awhile. It was then and then only that I determined on coming to the States. Once determined on I set about its execution, or rather my friends set about its execution, for I was in their hands, and indeed it is to them and not to any effort of my own that everything is due. This departure from Ireland was much more difficult and much more full of incident than the escape from prison. But I do not care to dwell on it now. I want to come to the object of my mission to America. You know by this time that it is to reconcile the parties here and to effect a union—such a complete union as would give us very speedily all that we want for the freedom of our land. I found the organization here torn asunder, and, as already said, all sorts of bad feeling among the members. But I still believe that, from what the people have shown to me since my arrival in the States, I can effect enough for all our purposes. (Cheers.) It will give me the greatest possible pleasure, and it will give Ireland great pleasure, and the men who are now pining in prison, and the men who are standing in the face of all difficulties at home; it will give them infinite pleasure to see the heads of the sections coming into this organization united once more. (Cheers.) As already said, I have made advances for that purpose, and so far as I recollect I have not as yet let fall one single word that could fairly hurt any of these gentlemen. I did expect that Mr. Roberts would have acted like Mr. O'Mahony. I believe it was patriotic and wise of Mr. O'Mahony to have given in his resignation, and I believe it would be patriotic and wise of Mr. Roberts to do the same; and if Mr. Roberts and Mr. O'Mahony passed on this platform to-day, forgiving one another, forgetting the past, stretching forth the hand of brotherhood one to the other, and calling on the men to work together—if they had been here to endorse me, I believe that the organization would have in a single month ten times the power it ever had, and that the liberty of Ireland would be a certain thing. (Voices. Down with them! pitch them overboard!)

MR. STEPHENS (emphatically)—I have already called on you not to say a word hurtful to anyone. I have a great respect for Mr. Roberts and Mr. O'Mahony, and for every man till he is proved to be dishonest, and, once proved to be dishonest, I am then done with him for ever. But nothing of the kind has been proved against any of these gentlemen, so you have no right to hoot at them, no matter who may have set you on. Here, publicly and before the Irish people, I once more in a friendly and fraternal spirit invite these gentlemen—the heads of all parties—to come to me while I remain in New York, and endeavor to come to an understanding. I call on the Irish people here and throughout the world—for I believe the words I pronounce, however simply spoken, will be read wherever our race can be found—I call, then, on our whole race to rise up against the man or body of men who would stand between Ireland and this essential union to-day. I appeal to you by all you hold dear, by the memory of that land so fair, so full of sorrows, and yet so stedfast, so resolute, so pure, and enlightened as it is to-day. For I claim for Ireland at this hour more true republican principles and lights than are to be found in the same number of people in any country on earth. (Cheers.) And if there be more anywhere else, it must be on this republican continent. But certainly, I do say this, and I say it deliberately—for I know that these words will be read in France and in other lands that are so very dear to me, for France I do love. (Prolonged and enthusiastic cheering.) I say that not even there nor in any other land in Europe is there so much republican intellect as in Ireland. I say that we are well worthy of liberty, and that we are able to win it, if you do not deceive, or rather if you do not disappoint us in any way. In fact I might let the first word stand, for indeed if you disappoint us then you will truly betray us. You must disappoint and betray us if you are not united. This unity of action is the grand essential to-day; you must labor for that, think of nothing else but that, and don't rest till you have effected it. (Cheers.) Countrymen and friends of Ireland, for very important reasons I shall not extend my address to you to-day, but through the press and elsewhere you will hear of me again. The last words I shall say to you now will be but a repetition of what I have already said. Without unity we cannot have what we require, and you cannot fulfil your promises to Ireland; the Irish people are sure to be disheartened and dispirited; the organization is sure to be broken up, and an eternal stain will rest upon our character; but, worst of all, the whole Irish race is sure to be exterminated. (No, no.) It is certain that the Irish people will be driven from the soil of Ireland if you do not free her. If there is not union I believe the whole movement will end in failure, and then the doom of your race will be sealed. Believing, then, that union is the great want of the present time, I have in many ways cut short this address to avoid any remark that might be considered fairly hurtful to any man. Once more, I repeat, I stretch forth my hand to any man who may come to effect this union; and I call on you now, in the name of Ireland, to allow no man to stand in the way of this unity. (Cheers.) Effect it, and as sure as I address you here to-day we shall take the field in Ireland this very year, and by effecting it we will have a free land. Brothers, as my object to-day is to endeavor to effect this unity, I deem it wise that no other gentleman should address you on this occasion."

Mr. Stephens then retired from the front of the platform amid deafening cheers and waving of flags and banners. During the delivery of the above address, which occupied about an hour and a quarter, the crowd listened with unusual attention and eagerness.

The address was not intended as an oratorical display at all, but merely as a plain unostentatious statement of facts, which should disabuse the brotherhood here, and the outside public, of some most erroneous notions they had imbibed with regard to the condition of affairs in Ireland, and especially concerning the amount of pecuniary aid that had been received from America. It answered its purpose admirably, and was received with great satisfaction by all those who had the most right to demand information, and who were the most deeply interested.

Mr. Stephens then proceeded to carry out his plans for cementing the fractured organization, which he and his advisers had arranged. It was thought best that he should make an extended tour throughout the country, addressing the brotherhod and the citizens everywhere, and making such expositions of Irish policy as it might be prudent to make public. Before proceeding on the trip to the more distant points, it was decided to deliver addresses in the cities nearer the great commercial metropolis. Accordingly, Mr. Stephens visited New Haven, Newark, Brooklyn, and other near-by places, in each of which towns he made a telling speech, being everywhere received with great enthusiasm, and many good wishes and promises of material aid. His oration was generally announced as an exposition of the "State and Necessities of the Cause of Ireland at Home and Abroad."

MEETINGS IN BROOKLYN AND COOPER INSTITUTE—QUESTIONS BY THE AUDIENCE AND ANSWERS BY MR. STEPHENS.

In Brooklyn, and also at a second large meeting in New York, Mr. Stephens adopted a novel mode of giving to the public the information so much sought for in regard to the condition of Ireland and the Fenian difficulties. After speaking to his audiences for a time, he requested any individual to ask him questions, promising to answer truthfully and fully any and all except such as would bring to grief the brave men at home. The following questions and answers are the most important ones elicited at these *séances*:

Q.—Do you think it possible to secure the liberty of Ireland without a fleet?

Mr. STEPHENS.—I believe it practicable to break the English power in Ireland without one ship. If I did not believe this, I should not be here speaking in behalf of Ireland. We have the power within ourselves to conquer our freedom.

Q.—Has the American Consul in Ireland done anything towards obtaining the release of American citizens arrested there for being connected with the Fenian movement?

Mr. STEPHENS.—The Consul has given the utmost dissatisfaction to every Irishman, and has lowered the dignity of the American Government in Ireland. He should be brought to a strict account for his conduct.

Q.—Does John Mitchel agree with your views regarding Ireland?

Mr. STEPHENS.—So far as I know, yes. He thinks we ought to wait till late in the year before fighting; but he knows nothing of the organization in Ireland, not having been there for eighteen years.

Q.—Was it through your influence that P. J. Meehan escaped assassination from the Irishmen in Ireland?

Mr. STEPHENS.—I have to say, that on three different occasions he was saved from a traitor's death by my influence. There is not a man in Ireland who does not believe that Mr. Meehan knew when and where he lost the documents. Those documents, simple in themselves, were the immediate cause of the arrests in Ireland last year.

Q.—Please to explain the nature of the documents lost by Meehan, and the people compromised?

Mr. STEPHENS.—That is as easy as A, B, C. The nature was that I was addressed as the C. O. I. R. (Sensation.) The British Government acknowledged that they could not have taken one step but for the discovery of those documents. They were the real cause of the arrests in Ireland. The British could not depend on Nagle; the Attorney-General said they had nothing certain till they received those documents. (A voice—"But only three men were mentioned.")

Mr. STEPHENS.—That was enough to cause all the arrests; they found out that they could learn more from the office of the *Irish People*, and so seized it.

Q.—Hasn't Napoleon III. the key of England in his pocket to-day?

Mr. STEPHENS.—Napoleon III. has been likened to the Sphynx, and the secret of his great power lies in the fact that he keeps his mind to himself.

Q.—Is Mr. Roberts in favor of a union of the Brotherhood?

Mr. STEPHENS.—Mr. Roberts is inclined, I am informed and believe, to look at things in a right way; to abandon ruinous projects; to do all he can to effect a reconciliation.

Q.—Did you not save the life of Sullivan Goula, whom Gen. Sweeny has lately cited to prove his popularity in Ireland?

Mr. STEPHENS.—But for an order issued by me and reiterated, that man would have died had he a hundred lives. Unfortunately Mr. Sweeny knows nothing of Ireland, not having been there for many years, or he would not refer to such men to prove his popularity.

Q —We here have subscribed one million of dollars; what has become of it all?

Mr. STEPHENS.—I can only answer for what has been received by me, and the total sum received in eight years is less than £30,000. The Executive Committee will give you their report of what has become of the rest in a few days.

Q.—Are Schofield and Nagle alive yet?

Mr. STEPHENS.—I think it just as well to leave a little mystery about these matters. Scoundrels of this nature will always receive their deserts. There is a determined spirit in Ireland to mete out to traitors a traitor's doom.

Q.—Have the men of the North (outside of those who are pledged to the Crown) shown any disposition to stand up for liberty?

Mr. STEPHENS.—The men of the North are second to no men in Ireland to-day.

Q.—Is there a prospect of union?

Mr. STEPHENS.—Some of the leaders are in favor of a reconciliation, and others will not have union at any price. I believe, however, that ere long we shall have a union of the masses, regardless of the leaders.

Q.—Do you think that the French people are in favor of the Fenian movement?

Mr. STEPHENS.—The French people love liberty wherever found.

Q.—What amount of army equipments did you get at Union Square, and how much do you want?

Mr. STEPHENS.—A fair and full answer to that question would be tantamount to the loss of my documents. I shall take all I want, and more if I can get them.

Q. In view of the obligation of our oath of naturalization and the rights and privileges American citizenship confers on us, is it good for our race, or in accordance with the plighted oath we have given to America, to cross the border and make war on the people of Canada?

Mr. STEPHENS.—It would be ruinous to our race. I believe that in acting in such a manner as to compromise this country you will be committing a crime. We have only to unite and have faith in ourselves, and we can do our own work without the help of even so good a friend as America. We must not compromise any country in our struggle. In regard to the oath, I believe it would be a violation of it for you who have taken it to cross into Canada.

Q.—Can you get artillery into Ireland? If not, can you fight without it?

Mr. STEPHENS.—I will undertake to get all the munitions of war we want into Ireland, in spite of all the watchfulness of England, if you will only give them to us. After a few days' fighting we should have several parks of artillery in our possession.

Q.—Do you think that the fact of a man emigrating to America absolves him from his oath as an I. R. B.?

Mr. STEPHENS.—I believe the oath to be binding on the soul of the man who takes it—to be binding until he dies or Ireland is free.

Q.—Can England claim the allegiance of a former subject who has been naturalized here?

Mr. STEPHENS.—England claims the allegiance of every man born on her soil, no matter whether he has become a citizen of any other country or not. The moment any one of you lands on Irish soil, England claims you for her own.

Q.—Did O'Mahony send all the money to you that was collected here by subscriptions and otherwise?

Mr. STEPHENS.—I cannot say how much of it I received. If you had several men collecting money at the same time, you would find it difficult to tell how much they got.

But, said a voice, O'Mahony blames the Senate for holding back the money. How's that?

Mr. STEPHENS.—O'Mahony and the Senate and all held back

the money and spent it for conventions, mansions, and other such foolish matters.

Q.—A lover of the ladies desires to know if the girls at home are *trumps* in the cause of Ireland?

Mr. STEPHENS.—The girls at home are not only *trumps* in the cause, but are the *ace* of hearts itself.

This novel method of arriving at the truth gave the utmost satisfaction to all parties, the questions eliciting facts which would not naturally have been touched upon in the course of a speech.

Mr. Stephens' work in America is not yet complete, but at this date bids fair to bring forth good fruit. If integrity of purpose, long suffering in the cause, and many noble sacrifices for the cause, deserve success, then will he be successful. His countrymen at home look to him as their deliverer, entrusting him with the destinies of their country, their fortune, and their lives. Let no Irish-American withhold from him that support which he solicits in the name of Erin's Green Isle.

THE END.

www.ingramcontent.com/pod-product-compliance
Lightning Source LLC
Chambersburg PA
CBHW020125170426
43199CB00009B/637